Foreword

Like so many entrepreneurs, I found myself in need of a real-life Bart Steele—the Velveeta-loving, fedora-wearing, beer-drinking genius of a business detective at the heart of *The Forecast Fatale*.

I had co-founded a software business that, after years of healthy growth, was facing the threat of stagnant sales. As successful as we were at starting and subsequently transforming a software services business to a software product business—something entrepreneurs rarely live to tell about—we were in new territory when it came to building, scaling, and maintaining a healthy sales enterprise.

Enter Brian Schlosser, a real-world Bart Steele.

I met Brian at an awards ceremony at which our company's product beat his to win the title of Enterprise Product of the Year. We may have had the title and the superior product, but we didn't have the sales to match. I took many months to lure him to our company, an accomplishment I still consider one of the greatest of my career. As you read this book you will see why. In part, it is because our sales have grown more than 200% under his leadership.

The scenarios in which Bart Steele finds himself are drawn from Brian's successful career as an executive, sales manager, sales professional, and a brief stint as an engineer before he realized that it was the allure of sales that really got him all charged up. This hilarious *noir* mystery is also a pragmatic how-to manual that imparts wisdom and knowledge through real-world examples and an actual sales plan, something every successful sales professional should have.

Bart Steele offers practical advice on topics ranging from assessing prospects to presentations. *The Forecast Fatale* is also a tear-jerker that elicits tears of laughter at Bart's escapades, tears of horror at the recognition of your own struggling company, tears of self-identification in the troubled sales professionals, and finally tears of joy that Bart saves the day.

If you don't already know the real Bart Steele, make it your mission to find someone like him — your organization will be the better for it, even if it hurts!

Elizabeth T. Miller, PhD.
Co-Founder & Chairman
DatStat Inc.

Introduction

All characters in this book are fictional. That means they are an amalgam of dozens of traits, situations, ideas, and phrases that I have come across over the years. Many people tell me that they recognize themselves in the book. If you see something positive then, yes - it was probably based on you. If you see something negative then, nah - it was definitely based on someone else.

I can't possibly thank everyone I've had the pleasure of learning from so, here is a short and incomplete list of people who taught me things that Bart knows: Ken Thorsen, Mike McCabe, David Proestos, Mick Erlich, Charlie Cox, John Walliser, David Tomlinson, Rich Floegel, Lewis Carpenter, Fordham Tucker, Steve Irons, Fred Monjazeb, Larry Jordan, Kathryn Hardie, Cash Elston, and Joe White.

Thanks to Lizza Miller for writing the foreword. I haven't read it yet but, she's really smart and nice and I'm hoping she doesn't trash Bart or me.

Ken Shear is a great friend and Libertary is a great organization. In countless ways, that is why this book is available. Thanks to Christina Kinnaman for managing the book and Lynne Anderson for doing the design!

Rachel Leach edited the book. She did a great job and helped me to understand the reader along the way. Any defects in the book are the fault of the clumsy author and not the talented editor.

My parents, Ken and Marie Schlosser, read early versions of the book. They have always believed that I can do anything I set my mind to; even when objective facts indicate they are profoundly wrong. I am forever grateful for their error.

When my wife read this book she cried. I thought I had considered every possible comment, reaction, or criticism my life partner might come up with. I didn't think of that one. Go wife!

Bart Steele is like me, but much better, in all ways except one: I have the support of my wife and daughters – Denise, Kristen, and Erin. They are why I'd rather be the author than the character.

And so…

Bart Steele, Business Detective

The Forecast Fatale

Brian Schlosser

~ Table of Contents ~

~ Bart Steele's Advice ~

Chapter 1

Dawn and a Difficult Man

The day was gray and wet in the city that seldom buys. I'd just slopped the morning's first latte on my Ernesto Calamari tie, and panic was setting in. I didn't have the cash to replace the tie, and the only way to get the stain out was to place it in a nuclear accelerator while still wet. While I was at it, my career could use some nuclear acceleration, too. If I didn't get an engagement soon, I was going to have to give up my luxury office space with its breathtaking view of the alley, squeaky floors, and icy draft. Worse yet, I might have to face getting a regular job. I'd probably just sell another kidney. You have three, right?

The phone startled me when it rang. I was preoccupied with feeling sorry for myself, and, truth be told, the phone doesn't ring all that often in my office. The woman on the other end had a voice that made me think of a slinky black dress, but she didn't seem happy to be making the call. In fact, she sounded like she had taken a bite of something nasty and was anxious to spit it out.

"I'm Ms. Oglethorpe from United Software Corporation. Our president has directed me to arrange for you to come over here right away. She has need of your . . . *services*."

Apparently the mention of my "services" was the nasty thing that she didn't want in her mouth. I decided to roll out the charm. "Don't get your karma all crumpled. I'll be right over, I'm pretty close." I assured her. "On second thought, give me an hour. I have to deal with a fashion emergency."

"That is no reason to keep our president waiting!" She gave the phone a good slam. I'm sure that people in Asia Minor felt the shock wave.

I tore my tie off and made for the door. United Software is the kind of client that I live for: big and famous, with a complex product, a long sale cycle, and cash to burn. I was sure I could help them, too. I know every trick in the book and every two-bit sales punk in the city. I'm dangerous with a laptop, and I could cut your heart out with my cell phone. There are a million deals in the city that seldom buys, and I know about every single one. My name is Bart Steele, and I'm the Business Detective.

Chapter 2

Fool Me Once

John is my haberdasher and part-time assistant. After the call with Ms. Oglethorpe, I rushed down to his shop on Central Ave. When John saw me come through his door without my tie on, he ran to the back and brought out the quality merchandise—the stuff that's too good for the clowns that blow in off the street.

John held up a tie. "Zeez is esquisito, Signor Bart! She has just arrived from Italia in zee case of lead. Before zeez very moment, she has never seen zee light of day! Zere is not another like it in zee entire world!" The tie was a work of art.

"Can the accent, John. I'll take the noose, but I won't pay for your verbal trip to Italy," I said firmly.

"Aw heck, Bart. I was just practicing on y'all. I wouldn't charge you full price. It is a one-of-a-kind, though," John countered. He had that raw-boned look that came from his hometown of Nowhere, Texas, but he could fake an accent like the best of them. It was a valuable skill that kept John in business.

"Stay sharp, pal. I got a job and I may need your help," I told him as I knotted my new tie and took off for my appointment. I could hear the start of some silly talk about payment as I dashed down the street.

On the way up to the office, I asked a guy in the elevator for Ms. Oglethorpe's first name. He looked a little sheepish and told me that he had never heard it used, but that he was pretty sure it was Denise. I guessed that the poor guy was scared to death of her.

When I reached the top floor, I introduced myself and pointedly called Denise by her first name. She immediately turned pink, but I couldn't tell if this was a girlish blush or the early stages of a stroke. Despite that, Denise looked pretty good for such a hard case: she had dangerous curves, and her soft brown bangs hung over intense brown eyes. I'm a sucker for bangs. After a few minutes of my witty repartee, Denise finally sat me down in the president's office to wait. "Don't touch anything!" were her parting words. She must have been a remarkably strong woman to resist my charms.

Chapter 3

United Software's Story

Everyone in town knew the basic story of United Software's new president and CEO. Kristen Archer had been vice president of marketing. She had a reputation as a strong manager and a great product visionary. She had cut the marketing budget in half and improved the company's position in the industry by implementing a vertical market focus and an insistence on measurable results. When the last president had decided to go to Tibet to contemplate his navel, the board didn't hesitate to turn to Archer. I had never met her and didn't know what she would be like in person.

Inside Kristen Archer's office, I took stock of my surroundings from my seat at the conference table. She had a regular office chair—not one of those astronaut chairs that software people go for. There were a few stacks of paper on the desk, but they didn't seem to be out of control. She also had a few pictures of her family lining the credenza, but she didn't appear in any of them. Could this be the office of a CEO with her ego under control? The only award displayed was for some kind of business leaders in the classroom program. I like to think that I can get a feel for a person by looking around their office, and it seemed to me that Kristen Archer might be all right. I waited.

She was even better in person. Archer strode into the room and offered a warm handshake. In her forties, she was attractive in that corporate way, with well-done makeup and honey-colored hair. Her eyes were the only unusual things about her appearance: they seemed to change color slightly from one moment to the next. They went from almost blue to green to brown, depending on the light.

Kristen Archer had style. She was comfortable with herself, and she made me feel comfortable being with her She was also very direct: "Mr. Steele, you have a reputation for being eccentric. You also have a reputation for being dedicated and discreet, and that is what I'm looking for. I know a few of your clients and they all say you helped them."

Then she told me her story.

"I took over as CEO about two months ago. Everyone knows that our previous president left on a journey of self-discovery. What they don't know is that he decided to go one day and left the next. I stepped in without any turnover. Our VP of sales wanted the top job, and when he didn't get it, he left. After his departure, I discovered that our sales had been unpredictable and declining for some time, and now it has really gotten bad. We have saved our numbers up until now with some big customer upgrades and unusually large orders. But we can't stay lucky forever, and because I'm new to the position, I stand to be blamed for the problem no matter when it originated. I've started a search for a new sales VP, but that will take a while, and that person is not going to have the same customer connections that helped the last VP pull in long-shot orders. I also don't feel good about bringing in someone new until I fully understand what the problem is and how I should go about fixing it. My background is not in sales."

"And that's where I come in?" I asked.

"Exactly," she replied. "I need you to find out what's wrong and tell me how to fix it. Help any of our sales folks that you can along the way. Keep a running log of what you find, and report back to me every few days. Let's get going."

I named my fee. Archer took me down by half without breaking a sweat. It was still more than I expected.

"It will be well worth the money if you can get to the bottom of this," she told me. Then she flashed a smile that was really more of a grimace and said, "If you can't, I don't suppose I'll be around to hear that I spent too much for your services."

I rose from my seat. "I'm on the case," I told her. "You *will* spend too much, but I guarantee that you're going to be around to explain why."

As I turned to leave her office, Kristen complimented my new tie. "I love it. In fact, I bought the same tie for my husband a few days ago, from a fellow with the cutest Italian accent down on Central. You should visit him." I assured her that I would definitely pay a visit to the man with the cute Italian accent.

Even learning that my pal John had played me for a sucker wasn't going to ruin my day. After all, I hadn't paid him for the tie. And I'd avoided regular employment once more. I remained the Business Detective.

Chapter 4

A Deal and a Cup of Pain

My first full day on the case was crisp and sunny. I was happy to get out of my office. I'm a sales professional through and through, and it always cheers me up to get out and meet people. The term "sales professional" is important to me, because sales is one of the most intense and difficult jobs in business. The select few who can do it well should behave like professionals and expect to be treated as such. I hoped that United Software had a staff of professionals.

It also cheers me up to have a paying client. I had stopped by John's store on my way home the previous afternoon, and was wearing another new tie (that I acquired after I calmly and rationally explained to John how difficult it would be for him to sell clothes with one of his mannequins protruding from his left nostril. In fact, that discussion went so well that my current fashionable neckwear was obtained without the need for remuneration.) Once my testosterone level had dipped below "Neanderthal," I arranged for John to use his different accents to call in to United Software and request information a few times. He would keep track of the responses he got. I hoped none of them included a restraining order.

Every sales professional needs a plan, and it works the same way for detectives. The first step in my plan was to get to know the product. Kristen had arranged for me to meet with the local sales manager. Rob Lazlo was a ten-year company veteran with a little bit of a paunch and tired eyes. He didn't seem too shaken by the prospect of me poking around; when your sales district is right at the home office, one more consultant is no big deal. Rob said he had a couple of sales people hosting prospects that day, and he set me up to be a fly on the wall in each meeting.

The sales person hosting the first meeting was Manny Rodriguez. He was a medium-sized guy in his late twenties who looked like he was in his late teens, but he dressed professionally and seemed likable. He had energy to burn, and was convinced that this prospect was going to be huge. I joined him for a coffee to find out why. More correctly, I joined him for a brown liquid composed of water, unidentifiable organic material, and the solvent used to remove the burned black crust from the bottom of glass coffee service decanters. I was considering some sort of hazard pay surcharge.

Manny started: "When you get a decent lead around here, you really have to dig in. This one looks good."

"Do you get a lot of junk?" I wondered.

Manny rolled his eyes, which I took to be a comment on the quality of United Software lead generation and not a toxic reaction to his beverage. "Yeah, we get leads. But nothing ever comes of them. Half the time the prospect doesn't know what we're talking about when we pitch to them because it's been so long since they inquired."

I took this in and asked: "Are you forecasting this one to close?"

Manny combined a look of utter sincerity with barely contained excitement. "Oh yeah, they should close in about a month and a half. I've got them rated at 65 percent, and I really feel good about them."

I took a sip of my coffee and immediately lost the feeling in my fingertips. "I can't wait to see your presentation," I told Manny as I looked for a place to dump my coffee without creating a toxic waste cleanup site.

Chapter 5

As Far as Clean Underwear and Exuberance Can Take You

Manny's presentation took place in the district conference room. After I was introduced to the prospective clients, I retreated to the corner of the room. The prospect attendees included a director, a manager, and a technical guy who kept glancing at his text messages as though he was willing one to save him from another sales presentation.

Manny knew how to run a meeting. He started by asking the group a little about their operation and what they hoped to achieve today. When the technical guy started going on about object properties and molecular weights, I thought I could help by hitting him with a chair. Instead, Manny told him about his staff of experts in nano-technology and gene sequencing, assuring the technician that he would have them call him to discuss medieval art history. Those may not have been his exact words, but Manny did a nice job in getting the meeting back on track.

Overall, Manny gave an impressive presentation. Here are a few of the things that I tell people about giving quality presentations.

Bart's Advice on Presentations

Your slide show is too long. I don't know how long it is, but I know you have too many slides. Can't you find *one* to take out?

Don't expect your audience to read. Shorten every list. Shorten every bullet or sentence. If you want them to read, give them a memo or product literature or *Finnegans Wake.*

Use custom graphics. Don't use the standard graphics that come with the slideshow program—everyone has seen them. How about a picture of your product? What about a product diagram? Someone in your marketing department has everything that you need. Go appreciate them for two minutes; you'll be surprised by how happy they are to help.

Didn't I tell you that your presentation was too long? Remove the picture of your corporate office. Everyone has seen an office building before. Does every slide help you reach the point of your presentation? Can't you find *one more* to take out?

Do the things that your mom told you to. Stand up straight, speak slowly and clearly, and don't fidget. Vary your tone of voice and move your hands a little. Get excited—you love this product! Pick out people in

> your audience and make brief eye contact (not too long, that's just creepy). Do this with the back of the room as well as the front. You should also wear clean underwear in case you get run over by a bus while giving your presentation and have to go to the emergency room.

Manny's presentation was short and to the point. I didn't recognize his graphics from the last fifty presentations I'd seen, and there were no more than three bullets per slide. I stayed awake for the whole thing because it was lively and animated. At the end of the presentation, Manny determined that his prospective clients needed to do a cost justification. He offered to create a proposal. He even determined that the director couldn't sign the deal, but that he intended to sponsor it with his boss, the VP, when the time came.

When the prospect left, Manny was elated. "I told you they were a great prospect! I've got the process figured out and I'm going to close them in six weeks. I'll move them to 80 percent probability." He was practically dancing.

I asked him, "Why six weeks?" and Manny's youthful exuberance didn't fade a bit.

"They're desperate for what we have, and a cost justification will only take a couple of weeks. After that we'll work through the closing process. We'll have the order even sooner than six weeks!" he chirped.

I started to ask about budget cycles and whether any money was allocated for this, but Manny had already gone off with one of his system consultants to talk about the impending cost justification. I'd learned a little about the product, and a lot about Manny. It was a start.

Chapter 6

Bull — Raging and Thrown

I pulled up an empty cubicle in the bullpen to wait for my next appointment. I've never heard of a human resources or accounting bullpen—I guess only sales is staffed by raging beasts that need to be contained. Like most sales bullpens, this one was organized with the most senior people near the windows and the junior people farthest in. The most senior sales people often spend the least amount of time in the office, but tradition and hierarchy are important to many of these organizations. The gray cubicles, florescent lighting, and the constant low hum of phone conversations reminded me of my early days in sales. I watched and listened to one of the junior people in the cubicle across from me as he worked the phones:

"Our product is an integrated software system. It provides enterprise-level financial benefits to mid- to large-sized organizations." He paused with his pen hovering over a notepad.

"Well, we do that by leveraging technology to control costs and integrate the data that is an important company resource." He paused again, and I could see that the prospect was starting to slip away from him. It was no wonder, with the meaningless crap he was spouting. Had I been drinking coffee, I would have tried to drown myself in it. "If I could just get a half an hour of your time, I could understand your business and explain how my company can help to maximize your profit potential." The prospect was gone now, but the salesman was fighting to the end.

"O.K. Thanks for speaking with me and if I can . . . ." The salesman hung up the phone.

For a second he looked like he might cry, but he immediately reached for another sheet of paper and started to prepare for another call. I wandered over to introduce myself.

"Hi. I'm Bart Steele. Sounds like a tough call," I said.

The thin, dark salesman looked up. "I'm Raj Patel. I've heard of you. You're that detective that our president hired. Am I in trouble?" He was joking, but I could see the tension in his face and body language.

"I'm a business detective, and we only make arrests in extreme cases. You know, like when somebody fills out their paperwork wrong."

Patel looked at me like he was pondering a decision and said: "Maybe you should arrest me for impersonating a sales guy. I'm getting nowhere with these leads."

"You haven't been with the company very long, have you?" I asked.

"Ouch! Does it show that badly?" Again, Patel was joking—but I could tell my remark bothered him. His inexperience did show pretty badly, but part of my job was to help where I could. I offered to help him if he wanted me to. He did.

I told Raj that he sounded good on the phone and that he seemed to have the guts for phone work. He asked if his Indian accent could be hurting his sales. I thought for a second, and then told him that his accent was very slight and probably even helped him a little. Raj beamed at that.

Raj seemed like the kind of guy who wasn't a natural phone person, but who wasn't going to let that stand in the way of his success: just my kind of sales rep! He told me that he was doing about half leads and half cold calls, and that he wasn't having too much luck with either. The leads were divided by territory, so Raj knew he wasn't being thrown the bad ones—he must have been doing something very wrong. I noted Raj's critical self-awareness—a very positive attribute in a sales person.

I could have told Raj exactly what he was doing wrong, but in my experience, when you tell somebody what they're doing wrong, they tell you why they aren't. This can lead to tense moments. In most cases, it does not lead to the person having a life-changing moment and thanking you for your wisdom, insight, and dashing good looks. In light of my experience, I took a different approach with Raj.

"Get yourself a small tape recorder and tape your calls. You don't have to tape the prospect side of the call, just your side. At the end of the day, listen to the tapes and pick out your best, your worst, and an average call. The next time I see you, we'll listen to what you have and figure out what to do." Raj thanked me and promised to record all of his calls starting the next day. He seemed like a nice guy. I hoped I wasn't too late.

Chapter 7

Words That Hurt
More Than Broken Bones

My next appointment was with the sales team's most senior guy, Dave Pelton. Dave had put up some big numbers in the past and, from what I'd heard, had all the tools to do it again. He was in his late twenties or early thirties—the age when the hair is just starting to thin and the waist is just starting to thicken. Dave looked like he had been involved in a sport that required determination and endurance during the season and orthopedic surgery in the off-season. He had the whole alpha male executive routine down pat. His look was well-to-do banker, with his sleeves rolled up and his tie loosened a carefully calculated amount. His clothes were good quality, but unusually conservative for a guy his age. He reeked of testosterone.

I once hired the famous sumo wrestler Moribono to be the featured guest at a sales kickoff. My marketing department decided that I should do an exhibition round with the guy to amuse the troops. I'm in good shape, but Moribono could have whipped me using only his ponytail. He picked me up by my diaper and gave me a wedgie that I nearly had to have removed surgically. I only escaped with my life by frantically reminding Moribono that this was only an exhibition round and offering him a bonus if he let me escape with my dignity. He pretended that he had pulled an earlobe and I declared it a draw. The crowd went berserk. While they all told me that it was the greatest kickoff they had ever been to, I made a mental note to hire some analyst dweeb with a bow tie for the next year — and have him wrestle a marketing director.

Shaking hands with Dave gave me that same fight-to-the-death feeling. He flashed me a hearty and relaxed smile as he tried to crush the small bones in my hand and steadily pulled me toward him to make me feel off balance. Unfortunately for Dave, he was no Moribono. I held my balance and returned his smile, but not the extreme hand squeeze. Nothing throws a guy like that off like not reacting.

Once the physical ordeal was over, Dave and I chatted for a while. I learned that he was in the running for most total lifetime revenue with United Software, and that he had his MBA. Neither item came as a big shock to me. I was going to sit in on a meeting with a prospect for a pretty big deal. He knew his prospect inside and out. There was no bluff or bravado in the way he approached his customers. He told me things that could only have come from the prospect's highest executives. He met with them regularly, and had earned their confidence by working hard and providing valuable insight.

When we talked about the day's meeting, Dave was expansive. "We're meeting with the selection committee for the formal presentation of the solution. They already have the proposal, and the decision is due by the end of the month. Contracts are the month after, and I have already talked to them about what they want in the agreement. There is nothing we can't deal with. There are two other viable proposals from competitors, but one is way over-priced and the other has the potential for serious performance issues. I've got four of the seven votes on the committee already, including the leaders. I'm also on excellent footing with the executive vice president that takes the recommendation."

I was impressed. "Sounds great. How have you forecasted them?"

For the first time Dave seemed a little evasive. "Well, you never *really* know until your sale closes. Anything could come up. I've got them at 20 percent right now — I'm not ready to move them up for a while."

The prospect group started to arrive. Every one of them was exactly as Dave had described them, and Dave himself relaxed. He didn't act competitive with them, as he had with me. This guy had talent. He didn't go with a slide show; he had printed his graphics on poster-sized paper mounted on foam boards. The effect was to make the meeting feel more like an executive briefing and less like another vendor pitch. I could tell that the prospects liked it. When they did challenge him on a point, Dave handled the objection without sounding defensive or condescending.

Dave probably spent more time talking than I would have liked, but it seemed to work with this prospect group, who seemed genuinely interested in what Dave had to say. It was obvious that Dave had put a lot of work into getting the prospect to this stage. In fact, when questions came up about the specific requirements in their Request for Proposal they seemed to defer to Dave. I smiled to myself: I had seen this tactic before. It was one of the things that I try to teach whenever I can. When the meeting ended, I got a minute with Dave to confirm my suspicions.

"Dave, how did this project get started?" I wondered.

"The prospect group's EVP formed a task force to look at the potential savings they'd get with United Software. That rolled into the selection committee."

That seemed like a reasonable scenario. "Where did the EVP get the idea to look at the project?"

Dave grinned from ear to ear. "Oh, I see where you're going. I gave him the idea when I talked my way in and got my first meeting with him. He liked my suggestion that there were savings to be had and bonuses to be earned. Then, when the task force and selection committee were forming, I was right there, armed with valuable information. In fact, a lot of the requirements that they came out with started with materials that I gave them. That's how I know so much about what they need."

Dave had "rigged" the bid. Not in an illegal or unethical sense—he just got very close to his prospect and kind of sold from the inside.

"So, naturally, you are in position to win the business," I said.

"Sure, everybody knows that it's almost impossible to win business if you don't have a hand in the requirements early on. The prospects really don't understand what technology like United Software's can really do, and many of them don't want to use outside consultants. If you don't help them sort out what aspects of the technology are important to them, either another competitor gets in there and ruins it for you, or the committee pulls requirements from all over the place and the solution is unworkable. I help companies set up workable projects that will use my products to get them the best possible solution. By the time we're done, some of these people will get promotions because of this product."

Dave was sincere about what he was going to do for this prospect. He was as good a sales person as I had seen in a while, and I told him so.

"Thanks. It's going to be a great deal and make the company, the prospect, and me a lot of money by the end of the year." Dave's ego was starting to show itself again.

"But you're still showing it at 20 percent on the forecast?" I asked.

"Yeah. It's a sales guy thing. You've been out of it a long time; you might not understand."

I told Dave that I understood perfectly and let him try to break a couple more bones in my hand as we parted. It was late in the day, but Dave said he still had a few more hours of work to do. I had a commitment to meet John at our favorite watering hole. It's good to be a Business Detective.

Chapter 8

Good Night Moose

There was a dead animal's head hung up over the bar. It was a moose in a top hat. This was how the Elegant Moose Pub got its name. Nobody knew how the moose got there; it had come with the property when the owner, Sarah, bought it, and she hadn't bothered to get rid of it. Sarah was John's girlfriend. She came out from behind the bar when she saw me come through the door. At five foot ten with lustrous red hair, she looked hotter in a bar apron than most women did in the latest lingerie from Victoria's Secret. She managed the bar with an iron fist, and even though the clientele tended toward everything from lawyers and brokers to dockworkers, there was never any trouble at the Elegant Moose. My personal theory was that nobody misbehaved for fear that they wouldn't be able to come back and get another look at Sarah. Or maybe they were just terrified of her.

"Bart, baby!" Sarah gave me a hug so good it was illegal in ten states. "My sweetie is waiting for you in your regular booth."

"Sarah, the thought of an ape like John being anyone's sweetie has caused me to reconsider my plans to dine here." Her place made the best burger in town, but I wasn't about to admit it.

"Damn! I was counting on your reference to get me that third Michelin star." Sarah turned to go back behind the bar and I choked up at the beauty of the sight. I joined the large Texan and a basket of peanuts in the booth.

I filled John in on recent events, beginning with my frustration with Denise and concluding with the shot about my not being a sales guy that I had taken from Dave Pelton. John found this news quite amusing, and pledged to put Dave on his Christmas card list. He could see that I didn't find it nearly as amusing.

"Aw Bart, y'all feel an awful lot better after you've rubbed a little beer on it," he told me. He was probably right. I ordered a pint of wheat beer from a local microbrewery whose logo is a group of goats ice fishing. I cracked the shell off a peanut.

"Maybe this Denise woman doesn't like sales guys. Or detectives. Or business detectives, for that matter—I could certainly understand that," John continued.

"Never mind, John. I shouldn't have mentioned her. Forget I said anything. Did you make the calls?"

"Yeah, here's the list." John passed me a list of companies and names marked up with notes on what was said during the call. "I did it just as you asked. I called different offices and tried to sound interested but not give any real qualifying information. If they asked me any qualification questions, I put them in the call notes. I used the names on the sheet and changed my voice for each one."

I scanned the list. "Did you really use 'Chuck Dickens' and 'Ernie Hemingway?'"

"Hey, it's boring work. A guy has to have a little fun. Now back to this Denise—let's ask Sarah what she thinks . . . ."

John and Sarah proceeded to offer me opinions on the love life that I didn't have for about an hour and a half. I did finally eat a burger—and it was damned good. I finally left the two of them to discuss my personal life without me and headed out the door, tipping my hat to the moose on the way out. That poor moose had to listen to every ridiculous conversation in the pub. The least I could do was be polite.

Chapter 9

A Woman for All Categories

A couple of days later, I spent the morning working on my word lists. I maintain three of these lists: words I like, words I don't like, and words that just confuse me. I add to the lists every morning when I get to the office — right before I do my tai chi exercises.

I had just placed "bellicose" in the like list and added "turgid" to the don't-like list when the phone rang. I didn't spill anything or lose control of a bodily function this time — I was getting used to people calling me. The caller said her name was "Ms. Oglethorpe."

"Hi, Denise! I'm glad you called," I said, with all the boyish enthusiasm I could muster. This was considerate of me, because had I used my normal throaty testosterone-laden bass, I'm pretty sure she would have immediately started to purr like a kitten. Given that she was probably at work, I thought it was decent of me to save her the embarrassment. Her voice stayed flat and she got right to the point.

"Despite my advice, Kristen would like to have lunch with you today. Are you available?"

I told her that I was, and we set the place and time. Before she managed to hang up, I asked Denise why she had advised the president against having lunch with me.

"Mr. Steele, I fear that the sight of you eating may be an image that will haunt my friend and employer for the rest of her life. I was only trying to spare her that pain. Good day." With that, she hung up.

A lesser man might have been ruined, but I am no ordinary guy. I am a sales professional, and one of the best at that. I love rejection. It is the thing that makes the weaker people go away. It is guidance that tells me the most efficient way to close the deal. Denise's shot at me had been somewhat unprofessional. That was progress: her defenses were crumbling.

I thought about her bangs. I looked back down at my three lists of words. I added her name to all three categories.

Chapter 10

Aromas, Good and Bad

Kristen Archer surprised me again. I was expecting a dignified restaurant, one with tablecloths and frequented by people who stopped by your table to say hello and mention that you *must* get together and talk about those business development opportunities. A place where everyone eats marketing food. "Marketing food," part of my personal Business Detective lexicon, consists of salad and adjectives. It's not simple plain greens — they're either "baby" or "spring;" and the dressing is "delicate" or "tangy." "Tangy" is in danger of appearing on the list of words I don't like.

In lieu of marketing food, Kristen Archer and I waited in line for green corn tamales and colas at a Mexican restaurant owned by a guy named Danny. He fawned all over Kristen like the maître d' at the place we didn't go to. I asked Kristen how she knew Danny so well, and she told me that she ate at his restaurant whenever she could and that she occasionally had him cater parties for her.

"I prefer food with taste whenever I can get it. I didn't think that you would mind," she explained.

I told her that I didn't, and we picked up our food. The tamales were incredible, but with Denise's insult fresh in my mind, I restrained myself from licking the paper basket that my lunch came in. I've got class—most of it's low, but I've got it.

"Bart, I've read the reports that you've prepared for me, and they're interesting. I can see some small changes we can make, like teaching basic calling techniques. But I don't see anything that explains our bigger problems with sales."

"No, we haven't figured that part out yet," I replied. "But we're learning some things and beginning to get some clues. It seems to me that your sales people are basically competent. Sure, I've spotted some problems, but nothing too big. I've gone into some companies and found a sales staff full of losers. I haven't seen that at United Software."

"Um, I can see that. We don't have too much turnover either. When we do have an opening, it fills pretty quickly."

"Right. From what I can see so far, you have a good team and a compensation plan that attracts and keeps people. I'll also point out that the product makes sense to your prospects and that you have been able to generate leads for your people to work with."

She frowned at my last statement. "Every sales person that you mentioned in your report complains about the leads the company feeds them. I work hard to generate those leads, and it ticks me off that the sales people don't appreciate them." Her eyes were shifting color in the light. They got darker as she got angrier.

I sympathized with Kristen about the leads, but told her that this kind of problem is rarely about the leads themselves. After all, leads are just links to humans who want to know more about the product. How can they *not* be better than cold calls? I suggested that some of the company's problems could stem from individual issues, like the one that I had uncovered with Raj. United Software's sales training needed an upgrade that emphasized the tying of product features to customer functions and the benefits to the buying organization. I also told Kristen that I thought there was more going on at United Software. We agreed that I would report my conclusions and recommendations in a week—she didn't think she could wait much longer than that to address the problem. We got up to leave the restaurant.

Kristen's cell phone rang and she took the call. Her assistant was calling to tell her about an employee who had been giving off a particularly foul odor. When his manager had asked him to fix the problem, he had gone to the HR department, made them all nauseous, and threatened a multi-million-dollar lawsuit under the new *Americans with Aromas* act. Kristen dealt with the emergency wearily. She saw me smiling and sternly pointed out that this was a serious HR issue and it was certainly not funny, but her eyes didn't get dark like they did before. After we parted on the street outside of her building, I was pretty sure I heard her laughing—which was incredible, considering the pressure she was under. If I could tell Kristen Archer what United Software's sales problem was and how to fix it, the company would be just fine.

Chapter 11

More Confusing than a Dead Guy's Math Homework

I never should have set out to prove Fermat's Last Theorem. It's no wonder that the thing had killed the old mathematician—it probably frustrated him to death. The day after my lunch with Kristen Archer started out bad and got worse. For one thing, I'd pumped up too much from my one-handed pushups. The added bulk in my biceps made my suit jacket hang badly. Always a perfectionist at fitting suits, John had measured me to the micron using a laser calibration device and, if my size varied by even a fraction, the whole look was ruined. I was too muscular by an inch and I didn't know what to do about it. If it weren't so disgusting I'd take up smoking or watching hours of reality TV to ruin my physique.

I am nothing if not dedicated to my clients, so I put aside the solution to Fermat's Theorem and my excessive muscle dilemma. I planned on spending the day following up with each of the employees that I had met and checking in on their deals. First on my list was the district manager who set me up with the sales reps. I was off to see Rob Lazlo again.

Rob was the tired-looking sales manager that Manny, Raj, and Dave reported to. He'd put me in touch with his sales team, but he and I hadn't spoken much. It was time for me to gain an understanding of what he was up against. Rob had been a successful sales person with United Software. That gave him credibility with the field and clout with management. He had been the district manager for about three years, and his record was spotty. He had some stellar quarters, and some total bombs. Kristen told me that Rob's core problem was the same as the rest of the manager's: he couldn't predict. Whether he was going to hit big or miss totally seemed to be as much of a surprise to him as to everyone else. I started our conversation by asking him about the sales people he introduced me to and how they were performing.

"Manny has done a couple of deals." Rob started. "They were good, profitable deals. He seems to 'cry wolf' a lot though."

I asked him to explain.

"Well, every prospective deal he takes on he forecasts at 100 percent. Our technical people think he does that so that he can monopolize resources. I think he's just too enthusiastic. I try to filter his projections before they make it into the official forecast but he has fooled me a number of times. Either I let him rate something high when it doesn't stand a chance, or I knock down the rating on a deal that winds up closing. Not that I mind getting deals; it's just hard to sort out what's feasible and what's not when he truly believes that every deal is 100 percent."

I asked how he was filtering what went into the forecast.

"For a while I was arguing with him on every deal. The guy never gives an inch. He's a true believer. Now I take every deal down by at least 20 percent—40 percent if I haven't met the customer. It seems to be the best I can do with him."

I wondered if Manny was a keeper. Rob thought that he was. It was hard to find people who could close deals, even if they did walk around seeing the world through rose-colored glasses. Then I asked him about Raj.

"It's really too early to tell with Raj. Nice guy, and smart. But he's still forecasting deals at 30 percent or lower. I really can't tell anything about the deals until they hit 50 or 60 percent because I don't have enough experience with him. He's really high on the calling help you gave him, though. I hope it works for him."

After we talked about Raj and some other new sales people for a few more minutes, I turned the topic to

Dave. Rob told me that a big part of his job was managing prima donnas, and that Dave was certainly in that category. He put up big numbers, but he refused to accept help, and he would never forecast a deal above 50 percent until he could see the first part of the purchase order coming through the fax machine. Dave was Rob's friend, but he sure made a tough job tougher. Finally I asked Rob what his biggest headache was.

"Bart, each of my ten sales people spends one to two hours a week scrubbing his or her accounts for the forecast. I review the forecast account by account with the sales reps. My management does the same with me, and then sales administration questions every account on top of that! Between the sales rep reviews and the executive reviews and the going over from sales administration, I must spend at least eight hours a week on forecasting. And we have a sales force automation system! Those meetings are brutal. Could a 70 percent deal be an 80 percent deal or a 60 percent deal? Sure it could. I'm making a judgment call that everybody second-guesses. Even with all that, I can't say that we are very good at it."

Rob gave me plenty to think about. Maybe he wasn't tired, but frustrated. I got a copy of the forecast that he sent to sales administration from him and thanked him. Fermat had nothing on United Software.

Chapter 12

Of Druids and Orange Cheese

I solved Fermat's Last Theorem on my way to sales administration. I ducked into a cubicle to enter the solution into my smartphone. I was very pleased; the thing had stood unsolved for three hundred and fifty years, and a mere Business Detective was able to wrap it up. Compared to that, solving United Software's sales problems would be trivial. Of course, I still hadn't solved the sales problem, and I hoped the folks at sales administration could help.

When I got there, an admin explained how the individual forecasts were rolled up into a national forecast using a procedure originated by druids in the twelfth century. In fact, during the course of the conversation several monks in hooded robes wandered by, carrying the sacred forecast scrolls. Once the forecasts were rolled together, various weightings and calculations were performed to yield a series of numbers that, when tortured, would admit to anything. While United Software's process was complicated to the point of taking on mystical qualities, I had seen variations on it performed at dozens of companies. When I inquired as to its accuracy, I drew blank stares. Eventually, the admin staff admitted that it hadn't been very good lately.

I gathered the sales administration version of the detailed and summary forecasts and left the area before the various incantations being recited there summoned a demon from the netherworld. I had enough to think about for one day, so I headed home.

At home, I got on the Internet and discovered that some guy from Princeton had already solved Fermat's Last Theorem. I deleted my solution from my smartphone and wondered if the world was truly running out of Big Questions to answer. I decided that I wouldn't take on another big problem until I had United Software back on track. I liked Kristen and all the people there, and I wanted them to be successful. It would take an empty brain—sort of.

I had worked myself into an awful mood. I reasoned that I'd be bad company as a dinner companion and decided to stay in and work on the sales problem. Dinner was an issue. My refrigerator is kind of a tasty United Nations. At any given time I may have smelt roe, cheeses from animals that have never uttered a "moo," and mushrooms that will only grow in zero-gravity environments and must be sniffed out by the trained snouts of astronaut pigs. I passed over about a thousand dollars worth of unpronounceable vegetables and bizarre animal products and decided to make an omelet with the soft orange cheese-related food that comes in a big block. It's embarrassing to admit, but I love the stuff. I sat down with the omelet, a big glass of milk, and a notepad to review what I had learned about United Software.

1. United Software's forecasts were unreliable.

2. Management saw declining results, but the forecast wasn't helping them see what was causing them.

3. The problem arose at the first level of management. The district manager could not predict his own performance any more than sales administration could predict the company's.

4. Some sales people were having difficulty getting accounts to a level that they could forecast at. (Raj.)

5. Some sales people were mis-assessing their opportunities. (Manny.) This was creating a problem in allocating resources to help the deals close.

6. Some sales people were purposely downgrading their opportunities in order to manage company expectations. (Dave.)

7. The company did not seem to be teaching a "feature-function-benefit" approach to presenting the product. Instead they were just listing benefits.

8. The sales people complained about the leads from marketing, even though, in my opinion, those leads appeared to be solid.

I stared at my list until my eyelids started to droop. I wanted to find a clear and simple solution, but everything seemed to be broken. I fell asleep at some point and, in the morning, found my plate stuck to the side of my face by the same orange cheese-related food that had been such a comfort the night before. I wasn't sure of anything, but I was convinced that I was on the right track. I pried the plate from my cheek and got ready to take on the day.

Chapter 13

A Phone is a Fortune

A couple of days had passed since I'd given Raj, the sales rep with the phone problem, his assignment. I'd waited longer than we had agreed on, but I'd done that on purpose in order to give him a little more time to work on it alone. I had him pegged as a sharp and hard-working guy and it was time to see if I was right.

I put away the origami crane I was working on. Most people don't realize how difficult it is to make those little back-bending knees. It's especially difficult if you don't follow a pattern and help the paper become the crane naturally. But that's another topic.

I grabbed my coat and hat and legged it over to United Software. The wind was blowing, and everyone I passed was squinting to keep the dust from the street out of his or her eyes. I tried to think of a wry philosophical observation about the world that I could draw from the sight of all those squinting people. It troubled me that I couldn't think of one—I usually do "wry" pretty well.

Denise Oglethorpe was coming out of the lobby store with a couple of soft drinks when I entered the building. I wondered aloud if the second one was for Kristen Archer. "Ever the detective, Mr. Steele," she replied. She tossed her hair and ducked into a closing elevator, leaving me standing in the lobby. "Call me Bart, please," I mumbled to the closed doors. I had a hollow feeling in my chest that told me that this relationship was beginning to get out of hand.

Raj was a lot easier to deal with than Denise had been.

"Mr. Steele, you have turned my career around. I can never repay you. You are a genius!" The guy was gushing. I hate gushing.

"Raj, chill, buddy. While I would never dispute such a fair and accurate assessment of my intellectual capabilities, I'm forced to ask: What did I do?"

This hardly slowed him down. "Your technique! I listened to myself for a couple of days. I got three appointments today," he enthused.

I told him how happy I was, and asked what he had changed about his calling. That stopped him in his tracks.

"I don't know. I was so happy to get a little success that I didn't even think about it. Do I need to?"

I explained that he was at risk of going back to his old mistakes if he didn't understand the improvements that he had made. We went into a meeting room to review the tapes.

First we listened to one of his early tapes. It went just like the conversation that I'd heard the other day. Raj spouted garbage about how good his product was; the customer asked what the product was; Raj spouted more stuff about increasing ROI and leveraging investment. Finally, the prospect got fed up and got rid of him. Sometimes they were nice; sometimes they weren't.

Raj looked uncomfortable when I made him listen to a later tape. Then we talked about it.

"So what do you think?" I asked.

Raj surprised me by acting dejected. "I guess I wasn't as good as I thought. I sold the benefits a lot more in the first tape."

I told Raj that it was true that he had spoken almost exclusively of the benefits at first—but that approach had failed! The second approach had succeeded. I didn't think it was a coincidence.

"But Mr. Steele, in the second tape I talk about features of the software and what it does. It's technical stuff that prospects don't care about. They care about the bottom line."

I told Raj that prospects do indeed care about the bottom line. "And they want to know *how* you are going to get them that benefit," I explained. "Remember, the phrase is *feature-function*-benefit.

Marketing and sales trainers always emphasize the 'benefit' part because a lot of sales people forget to include it, but it's just as bad to forget 'feature' and 'function.' You make it sound like your product doesn't have any substance, and that's why prospects get frustrated with you." Raj understood. He had instinctively found his biggest calling problem and fixed it; now he just had to make sure he got better and better. He asked me for other tips, so I gave him my guidelines for making first contact with prospects.

Bart's Advice for Prospecting by Phone

Treat every call like a cold call. Don't presume that someone who requested a follow-up contact knows all about your product or service. Ask them what they know and go from there.

Kiss a lot of frogs. Some will be princes.

Let the prospect know what you do and why he should care. A rejection lets you move on. That's not bad. An acceptance advances your relationship. That's better. Give the prospect the information to make that choice early. Remember, if they are a bad prospect, no amount of sales technique is going to change that.

Smile. It shows, even over the phone.

You're a pretty nice person; don't be afraid to let that show. Joke pleasantly and appropriately. You might mention how exited they must be to have a sales person call. If it sounds like a bad time for the prospect, set a better time.

If they aren't interested, ask who would be. However illogical this may sound to you, let it be known that you will one day encounter someone who does not want or need your product or service. But if they give you a lead, the call is not a total loss. It may even make them feel good to help you.

Record yourself. (But not your prospects without permission.)

Have a plan and plot your progress. Do this on a computer or on paper. The information you gather is valuable. You will be able to spot trends. Are certain types of businesses more receptive? You will be able to go back through old call lists and recall the ones that you think might be ready for you now.

Remember why you are doing it. Most people don't like making first calls. Motivate yourself. Is it to show your peers that you can do it? Is it to buy a car or to be your company's top performer? Put something on your desk to remind you of why you are making these calls.

Raj wrote all of this down and assured me that he would become the best new business caller that United Software had ever seen. I told him that I thought that he just might. It was time to leave. I put on my coat and hat and we walked out of the meeting room. I cut quite an impressive figure, but I don't think that was why I kept noticing sales people glancing over at me. Raj's success was spreading my fame.

"Hey Raj, one more tip. If you want to pick up some spare change, get a few tape recorders and rent them out. I think you may have started a trend."

Raj grinned from ear to ear. "I'm way ahead of you, Mr. Steele. There are three in my desk." His smile was contagious.

"Call me Bart, please." I left for lunch.

Chapter 14

Bart Learns From His Student

I had lunch with my old friend Fred. Fred was one of first sales people that I put in place when I became a district manager back in the Mesozoic period. Now he was a sales VP at another large software company. He was one of the best hires I'd made, and a highly intelligent man.

Fred came to me with enthusiasm and smarts and not much more. He made every mistake in the book. What made Fred different was that he only made the mistakes once. He learned quickly, and was fearless about confronting his mistakes. He was no longer a student—we were friends, and I had as much to learn from him as he did from me. The Sakura is a tiny, well-lit sushi bar on a side street downtown. It was our favorite place to meet because the owner was a fanatic about fresh food. Fred and I agreed that this was an important quality in a restaurant that served raw fish. I filled him in on United Software over tuna belly sashimi. Then we gobbled down some squid and talked about the challenges that Fred was having.

"I'll tell you, Bart, my biggest problem is with people who never learned the basics. I went on a call the other day with a sales person who has been around long enough to know how to run a call. She let it get away from her completely. Later she told me that she thought I was going to charge in and close it for her." Fred paused to load up on wasabi. He could eat more of the fiery green stuff than anyone I had ever seen. It didn't even make him sweat.

"Let me guess, she didn't do the ground work because she figured that your storied sales capabilities would carry the day," I said.

"You got it. No cost justification and no real qualification. The worst part was that the VP we met with didn't know that we were there to close and wasn't ready for it. But I didn't know that, so I started talking about the value of partnership and cost effective ways to purchase."

I knew from experience that Fred was very good on sales calls. This sales representative must have really failed to prepare him. I told him so.

"It's worse than that, Bart. The sales rep told me that we were going in to close. When the prospect realized that I wanted him to place an order, he got mad. He told me in no uncertain terms that his company wasn't going to place an order then, and that the final decision wouldn't even be his decision when they were ready. Finally, he told me that he resented my visit and that he was sure I had pushed the sales representative to let me try this inappropriate call."

I struggled to keep from blowing my soda out of my nose, imagining Fred taking a good chewing out from his prospect. I asked him what happened to the sales person, and he told me that she would never again make the same mistake. She now understood that there was no such thing as a "closer" and that the only way for her to close deals was to do all the necessary work. She would have to ask the qualifying questions and understand the prospect's buying process. Very often, she would need to help the customer evaluate the costs and benefits of her product. In short, she would have to handle all the basics in order to prepare her prospect for the close.

"I went on another call with another sales person the next day. This prospect *was* ready to close," he went on. "The problem was that the salesperson wasn't ready. It got kind of ugly."

I have to admit that hearing Fred's troubles took my mind off my own problems. "What do you mean, ugly?"

"He froze. The VP we called on said that they were ready to go and asked my guy what the next step was.

It took him by surprise—the whole team looked at him and he didn't say a thing. He just turned red and looked like he was going to pass out. I found out later that he hadn't expected to close, so he hadn't prepared for it. He wasn't ready with contracts and, since he was new, he didn't even know what to say about the process."

"That seems kind of silly." I told him. "Why didn't he just say that he'd get back to them?"

"You would think he'd do exactly that, wouldn't you? But he didn't. I guess he just panicked. The reason that he panicked and the reason that the other sales person botched a perfectly good deal is the same: neither sales person did the basics. They both operated as though the deal would take care of itself. One thought I would perform magic tricks, and the other didn't prepare for the next step in the deal. Pretty sad, huh?"

"You're right, Fred—that sounds ugly. What happened when the sales guy froze?" I wondered.

"I bailed him out, of course. Just like you did for me when I was a pup. Object lessons are fine, but I wasn't going to slow down a deal. Afterward the sales person and I talked about the importance of being prepared and performing all of the steps to closing a deal. It always comes down to the basics. When you fix United Software, you'll find the answer in the basics, too."

I thought that Fred was probably right. He had turned into a very good VP. United Software never would have gotten into the trouble they were in with Fred as VP. Now I needed to figure out which of the basics they were missing and how to fix the problem, fast. I barely remember saying goodbye and arranging our next lunch. Fred had me thinking. I needed to spend some more time with the folks at United Software.

Chapter 15

Timing is Everything

I hadn't seen Manny since his presentation, so I decided to check up on him. I found him at the tail end of a pretty tense exchange with the branch technical manager. It seems that she didn't think it appropriate to assign resources to one of Manny's prospect accounts. Manny was arguing that the account wouldn't close without the resource. Unfortunately, her position was that it wouldn't close with the resource, either. Manny made it a point to describe a few of the flaws in her operation, and it was decided that Manny would take the issue to Rob, the district manager. For a while I thought the exchange might come down like an episode of the *Jerry Springer Show*, but in the end everybody maintained control. Manny and I went to the break room and he offered me coffee.

"No thanks, my gastroenterologist threatened to sue for custody of my epiglottis if I touch that stuff again. Don't you think it's dangerous for you to have a stimulant right now?" I asked.

"Nah, that was nothing," Manny said. "I can't seem to get a damned thing done around here without throwing a fit. The company just doesn't seem to want to do business. It's not just the technical folks. The leads are junk, nobody pays attention in contracts—it's very frustrating." The flush was slowly starting to fade from his face.

"How do you think it happened?"

"Well, the old president always seemed like he was in another world. Our VP would beat the stuffing out of us for numbers, but nobody paid attention to what it took to do business. Now a lot of the departments are lazy, and people think that's the way it's supposed to be. The only way to get what you need is to go berserk. It's not like I'm a jerk; I don't want to throw a fit. I really don't have any choice. I'll tell you, it's wearing me down. I don't know how much longer I can take it."

"Any chance that she has a point about the likelihood of the deal closing?" I asked.

Manny smiled. "Sure she does, but the odds are always against a deal closing. I say it's a good deal and she says it isn't. How do we really know? I fight for my deals, and if the company doesn't back me, then I might have to leave. I'd like to see them try to get deals with the bureaucrats deciding what's a valid prospect and what's not."

"Let me change the subject, Manny. How is that deal that I sat in on last week going?"

"Pretty well. They are making progress on the cost justification and they are letting us help them. I had to push them to start working contracts with us, and we still haven't gotten them into legal. I'd still say we're on track for a quick close."

"Why did they resist working on contracts?" I wondered.

"I don't really know. I had to lean on them pretty hard to get it moving, though."

"Manny, I'm pulling for you on this deal. I noticed something that I think you ought to check out. It might be important, and it might not. Can I tell you about it?"

His forehead wrinkled. "Sure, go ahead."

I told Manny that I understood that there was money for the project that his sale was based on, but I hadn't heard anything about a specific timeframe. I told him that I was worried that, if there was a longer time frame than he expected, it would explain why the prospect's managers didn't see the urgency in getting going with the contracts. Finally, I asked him if he had had a specific discussion about timing with the prospect VP.

"Bart, I'm sure . . . ." He paused and stared off into space. "No, I haven't. Man, I hope you're wrong. But I appreciate the help. Rob tries hard, but we don't get that kind of thinking about deal strategy much around here. I see the prospect VP tomorrow. I'll make sure that timing is on the agenda."

Manny had his issues. He was one set of bad habits on top of another. Underneath it all I saw a dedicated guy who cared enough to fight for his deals, even if some of his ideas were a little misguided. Of course, if you viewed them in light of the current state of the company, his ideas were *not* misguided. They were just the best adaptations he could come up with to fit a work environment that was not good for doing his job.

Before I left Manny, I told him that I had heard that Denise Oglethorpe went to school. Did he know what she was studying? He said that someone had told him that it was something like medieval literature, and that she was working on her PhD.

"Raj told me that you were interested in Denise. He wanted to start a pool on you. The only problem was that nobody would take your end of the bet," he said with a smirk. "Take the bet, Manny. My forecast is never wrong."

Chapter 16

Insight Smells Like Hops

That night I sat with John over beverages at the Elegant Moose Pub. The place was spotless, but it still smelled like stale beer by the end of the day. Some people don't like the aroma, but it smells like home to me. My beverage of choice was a local microbrew that was delivered in specially constructed vacuum barrels made exclusively from super-conducting carbon nano-tubes. John had a Schlitz. Sarah was busy in the kitchen, so she couldn't torture me with questions about my love life. That was convenient, as I didn't have one. On the other hand, it meant that I couldn't see Sarah and was left to look at John's short red hair and linebacker body. He was a tragic example of what happens when you try to stuff an American body into an Italian suit. Life is full of trade-offs.

I told John about my discussions with Raj and Manny as well as Fred's belief that the solution would turn out to be about the basics. I told him that I saw a lack of leadership at United Software, and that the sales people appeared demoralized. Manny had come right out and told me that he was getting frustrated enough to leave the company. Raj didn't seem like he would leave voluntarily, but he might not have a choice. If my advice didn't help him make some progress, the company might let him go. I told John that I thought that would be a loss.

"Y'all turning soft in your old age, Bart? You know as well as I do that a lot of sales puppies don't make it."

"Yeah, but this one has what it takes. He's smart and aggressive and willing to learn. I'd hate to see him fail."

"Doesn't he have a manager?" John asked.

"Yup. That's what makes it difficult." I told him about Rob. "In the end, he's not that bad. He's been around and he knows the business. His team seems uncoordinated, though. They can't figure out how to deploy resources, and their forecasting is unreliable."

"That sure sounds like a management problem to me."

"I think it is, but the problem is bigger than a local sales manager. Kristen tells me that this district is typical. My instinct is to blame the last VP and maybe the famous navel-gazing former president, but that doesn't say much about fixing the problem."

"With those boys gone, it sounds to me like you've fixed part of the problem already," John offered. "I got the results on those test calls that I made. Maybe they will give you a clue."

John pulled out his notes and I opened up the forecasts that I had collected. I can't say that what we saw was surprising. John had made 25 calls to offices around the country. He had posed as a plausible prospect for their technology. He didn't lead them on or say he was a prospect; he just left a message asking for a callback from a sales person. Even though John was cautious not to consume anyone's time with his bogus inquiries, we felt a little uneasy about the ethics of this test. We'd both spent a lot of time as sales people, and we didn't like to lead them on. If John got a callback, he listened to the pitch and then quickly disqualified himself as a prospect. It wasn't pretty, but it told us about United Software's operation.

Seventeen of John's 25 calls were returned within two days. Three of those were callbacks from office staff. That was a little bit unusual. When John asked why a sales person didn't call, he was told that they didn't know who to assign it to.

This pointed again to management—there didn't seem to be a clear and universal understanding of territory. The result was that United Software was making its internal issues a problem for its prospects and customers. It also explained why John didn't get called back one hundred percent of the time. As disturbing as this information would be for Kristen, I was more troubled by what turned up when we cross-matched John's calls with the forecasts that I had rounded up.

Six of the 17 calls that were returned appeared on the forecast as prospects. None should have. Three were ranked at 40 percent on the raw forecast. Worst of all, two were promoted to 50 percent prospects on the national forecast—the version that was scrubbed by sales administration. To cap it all off, one inquiry that never got a call back made it all the way to 50 percent on the national forecast. Numbers, when tortured, will admit to anything.

"What do you think of these findings, John?"

"The sheriff should be takin' the part of the hound dog that goes over the fence last and makin' it the part that's headed over first," John twanged in reply.

I took a swig of my beer and thought about that for a while. Finally, I gave up. "How about trying that in American, Howdy Doody?"

"The boss needs to kick some hiney."

This kind of keen and complex insight had always been John's specialty. I couldn't say he was wrong. I decided to change the subject a little. "When they did call you back, how was the pitch?"

"Remember when you made me read that book of Japanese poetry? The stuff that didn't even rhyme?"

John brought this up at every opportunity. My one book recommendation, this small injection of culture, had left a festering psychological wound that even time could not heal. I told him that I remembered.

"Their pitches were almost as bad," John declared, spitting out his words as though the pitches constituted an affront on all that was good and decent.

I sighed. "Well, we knew they needed some work there. I must say that it is a joy hanging out with you."

He swallowed about a quart of Schlitz in one Texan-sized gulp.

"John," I said. "Nobody in Texas can spell Schlitz. In fact, before I met you, I thought it was extinct. Why do you drink the swill?"

"It's in memory of a woman I dated, a lovely girl. She was a steel worker. They all drink Schlitz."

"I'm sorry. How did she die?"

John stared deep into his malt liquor. "She didn't die, she dumped me. She was a strong woman, but not all that bright."

I wasn't prepared to fully evaluate his lost love's IQ, but that move seemed to speak well for her. "Does Sarah know the story?"

"Yup, when I told her she laughed and said that if she ever dumped me I'd have to start drinking champagne.

When I told her I hate the stuff, she said that was more reason to keep her happy. Now she keeps a bottle on ice. She's a hard woman, too."

I laughed. "If word gets out, guys all over town will send her cases of the stuff."

"Who would she get to wash her bar glasses for her?" John mused. "Hey, feel like doing some honest labor for a change?"

John and I ended the evening cleaning Sarah's bar while she worked in the kitchen. I said goodbye to Sarah and John and shrugged on my coat. On the way out I tipped my hat to the moose, as always. He declined to reciprocate.

Chapter 17

Money Talk

The day dawned clear and cool in the city that seldom buys. I did about forty minutes of tai chi on my balcony as the sun came up. It was chilly, but I didn't notice as I dismissed the physical world in favor of the spiritual one and found my center. It was pretty much where I had left it. I breakfasted on the healthful Malaysian bala-bala fruit, which tasted like one might imagine freshly-worn socks would taste. I washed it down with a bowl of Captain Crunch. There is only so much karma crap a tough detective can take. Even me. I got to the coffee bar a few minutes before Dave. I knew I shouldn't let his crack about not being a sales guy bother me, but it did. He knew I had been a sales guy, and he probably knew I had a pretty good reputation. And despite the crack, I liked Dave. He was smart and direct and aggressive. I'd arranged to meet him away from the office in an effort to lower his testosterone level and try to get him to talk straight. My guess was that he spent a lot of time thinking about what was wrong at United Software and had some pretty good ideas about what should be done.

He entered the café brisk and businesslike. His handshake was still a little too firm, but at least this time he didn't act like he was going to pee in every corner of the room to mark his territory. He was dressed casually, with a sweater over his shirt and dark khaki slacks. He looked the picture of a successful roll-up-your-sleeves businessman. Even his thinning hair added to the look. I asked him how his deal was.

"Coming along according to plan. They should select us by Friday. I'm on guard for trouble, but we are on track."

"Still forecasted at 20 percent?" I asked.

"Hey, I know I was kind of rough with you on that the other day. I shouldn't have been. I'm sorry."

This floored me. Dave was the last guy I would have expected to apologize for a minor insult, but I guess it fit. He was direct and fearless in conversation; he must be that way in evaluating himself as well.

"No problem. Does this mean you're paying for coffee?"

Dave grinned. "No. I didn't say I wrecked your car or ran over your dog. Don't detectives have expense accounts?"

I told him that he had a good point, and that his insult was no big deal. I added that people usually had a reason for lashing out, and I wondered if he knew what his reason was.

"Yeah, it's a holdover from the management that left. I do some pretty good deals, and they started to need them a little too much. In my estimation, they weren't doing enough to bring the pipeline along. As soon as I would expose a deal with a reasonable probability on it, they would go crazy."

I nodded to him to go on. I practice the encouraging nod relentlessly. If Dave really got stuck, I might add a well-placed "hmm . . . ." I didn't use it yet, though, because it would be overkill.

"First they'd promote the percentage. There was no arguing with them. They did this to round out their forecast and make it look the way they needed it to, and it was not reality-based. Rob tried to help me argue, but he's just a district manager; they ran right over him. Then they'd start putting time pressure on the deal."

I interrupted. "You've been around the block. Don't execs always put time pressure on deals?"

"Not like this. They would force executive meetings where they would trot out big do-it-now discounts and try to corrupt the customer's buying process. It was a mess."

"Did it work?"

"No! I'd be building statues to those idiots if it did. There's a right time to encourage a deal. I understand that. These guys were doing it to deals that were nowhere near ready. I tried to argue with them, but they had no feel for the prospects. They just went ahead, no matter what." He paused to take a sip from his hazelnut macchiato. It was an embarrassing drink, but at least it wasn't one of those chai tea things.

"So what happened?"

"At first it just cost me some money. You know how hard it is to take back a discount once you have shown it to a prospect. The discount they offered became the new starting point in the negotiation."

"Time-based discounts are the worst," I added.

"You said it. All the prospect has to do is let the deadline pass, and then you're in trouble. In this case, the execs ultimately pushed too hard on a deal and I couldn't recover. The deal went away. After that, I got very careful about keeping a low profile. I guess it's a hard habit to break."

Dave's story made sense. Bad forecasting, no understanding of the customer buying process, and botched discounting were all major pieces of the United Software puzzle. We spent some time talking about discounts and how and how not to use them.

Dave understood most of the key issues in discounting. Here's what we talked about.

Bart's Advice on Discounting

It's like this...

Whatever your product or service, you will be called upon to discount it sooner or later. The customer's approach can take many forms, and so can your response. The request may come directly as a demand or indirectly as an obstacle to closing the sale. Your response can be a simple "no," a number, or a complex set of concessions and terms.

No matter what the request or how you respond, this will be the most risky, rewarding, and emotional part of your sale. I cannot know about your product margins or value points. I cannot know what authorizations you need to give on price. I do know that discounts are the result of the previous activities in your sale.

Your product or service has a value and a price. If that value is extremely high in the prospect's mind and the price is perceived as low in relation to that value, then you will rarely be called upon to discount. Your ability to resist the request for discount and hold your value will be strong.

There are many techniques to building the perceived value of your offering over the course of your sale — that process is what your sale and all the effort you put into it is all about. It is important to remember that you should focus on building value at every stage of the sale; that effort is the single biggest factor in determining your success in managing discounts.

Discount: Who needs it?

You do. The need to discount can be a signal that your deal has moved within closing range. Isn't that what you have been working for? Don't panic.

Your prospect needs it, too. Understand the situation your prospect is in. Are they up against a purchasing threshold? What is the purchasing authority of your buyer? Are they nearing their end-of-year? Are other products or services competing for the same funds? By knowing the answers to these kinds of questions, you will have a better chance at crafting an offering that meets the customer's needs.

Sometimes a customer will reveal what concessions they are willing to contribute in return for consideration. They may be willing to act as a reference or provide you with a case study for your product. If they are going to make enhancements or add-ons to your product, they may be willing to license them back to you. These things might have a value to your company. If you are faced with having to offer a concession to your client, you will have to convince someone in your company that it is worth doing. Your client can help you with the internal selling that you need to do to help them.

I can't hear you

Beware of belly-bumping. When a prospect starts to work on your price too early in the sale cycle, it might be a very bad sign. What they are often saying is: "I don't understand your offering, and I don't want to. I'd rather talk about what a tough guy I am and how I'm going to beat you up for a discount." This behavior reminds me of a belly-bumping contest. There are no needs to meet or mutual advantages to be gained; it's an exercise for the prospect's ego and doesn't lead to a deal.

The first thing I do when someone starts asking for a discount before they understand the product is to suddenly become hard of hearing. Many times, a discount request is an off-hand comment that goes away on its own. If the prospect pursues the topic, I might gently joke with him or her about it: "If you think that the discounts are going to be big, wait until you see the surcharges." Sometimes even a small joke will disengage their ego and let you get back to establishing whether your product is a good fit for them or not.

If losing my hearing and making a joke doesn't work, then I abandon all subtlety. I tell the prospect that I'll be happy to review pricing when the time comes, but that I don't want to do that until we establish that he or she actually wants the product or service I'm selling. Finally, you can always bring them up short by asking if they are ready to sign the order right now.

I know he knows, but he knows I know he knows...

Don't anticipate too much. I have seen many sales professionals get all the way to emotional meltdown over pricing before they ever show it to the customer. They are convinced that the customer is going to go berserk because the price is too high.

Sometimes they don't! Other times, you have to do some discounting. The best way to avoid a bad situation is to make sure you prepare the prospect by giving them an idea of the scale of the price early. Why surprise them? If this sounds like it contradicts the prior section - it doesn't! I'm not suggesting that you give out detailed pricing information early—but if you're selling diamonds, don't let the prospect expect cubic zirconium pricing. They will just be angry and you will have wasted a lot of time.

Ouch, that hurt!

Don't be stone-faced. Remember that discounting is an emotional topic. For some reason, many sales people react to the discounting conversation by freezing up. If the prospect makes a request, show them a response that matches your feelings about that request. Don't go ballistic and don't put on an act. If the request is reasonable, look thoughtful. If the request is out of bounds, look troubled. Remember that this is a difficult and stressful time for many prospects, too. If they don't get visual and verbal cues from you, they won't understand what effect their requests have had. They may even have trouble behaving in a way that gets you to an agreement.

Cash is so tacky

I hate discounts that come in the form of a percentage or a dollar amount. That doesn't mean that I never give them or that you should not. It just means that you should carefully review *how* you are discounting and look for better alternatives than cash. There are two factors that come into play when you are discounting: value and price. In order to make your strategy effective, you need to either raise value, lower price, or both. Assuming that your prospect has adequate funds available, you are always better off raising value. Here is why:

Imagine that you are selling a solution that is composed of products and services that your company provides. You are faced with a situation in which you need to give something to the customer in order to close the deal. If you give up a thousand dollars off your price, that money comes out of your company's profits, dollar for dollar. If, on the other hand, you offer the customer additional products and services that total fifteen hundred dollars with a margin of 50 percent, you have improved the deal for everyone. Your revenue stays the same, and your profits are two hundred and fifty dollars *higher*. Your customer has received a package that has one third more value than a straight discount. It's a transaction that everyone can feel good about.

At times, a cash discount just won't do the job. The business situation may be such that no reasonable price reduction will get the deal. Even in this situation, a non-cash incentive may help.

Imagine that your solution requires a thousand-dollar piece of customer-supplied computer equipment to run. Your prospect has told you that it will take two months to select and order that equipment. You could offer your prospect a thousand-dollar discount to take your product now. Depending on your company's accounting policies, this may not qualify as a deal for two months, even if your prospect accepts. Your prospect may not want to have a set of unused products lying around for two months anyway. If, on the other hand, you offer to give the customer the needed computer equipment at no charge, you're likely to see a deal. The customer is relieved of the need to acquire the equipment, and your company can put the deal on the books. You might be able to acquire the equipment at a lower cost and *save* money.

Take credit

Sales people fail to do this all the time. Let's say they re-quote a customer at a lower price and save them money. Perhaps they have passed on a price reduction or used a program discount, added something for free, or just taken a few dollars off the price. The problem is that when they re-quote, they fail to itemize the reductions so that the prospect can see the benefit that the sales person is bringing to them. Don't EVER let me catch you making this mistake!

It's not the fall, it's the sudden stop

If you have to give a discount to make a sale, try to get something in return. Do this even if you don't want what you might get. The reason is that some prospects get a little carried away with negotiation. If you have given concessions, they will just keep on demanding more until you say no. Then they will get mad at you. I favor a change to the Constitution that requires these people to be registered with the government and restricted from doing business. Until that comes through, your only defense is to make sure that you get a concession from your prospect when you give one to them. This will help to limit their demands, and will help to attach value to the concessions that you give.

Caution, time warps ahead

There is one condition that many sales people place on a discount that you should think about carefully. I'm referring to a deadline. Deadlines can be risky. If you offer an incentive to a prospect in an effort to complete a deal by a given date, what are you prepared to do about it if they can't make that date? Often, the prospect will still demand the concession, even if they haven't met your time demands. Before you place a deadline on a discount, consider that if it does not work out it could cost you the deal.

In closing . . .

Discounting can be tricky for both the sales person and the prospect. I can also be very exciting, signaling the late stages of a sale cycle. If you think carefully, develop a strategy, and try to do what is right for your company and your prospect, you're likely to gain a great customer.

After we discussed discounting for a while, Dave and I said goodbye. We'd really hit it off, and agreed to have a beer at the Elegant Moose soon. I was glad that I'd taken another shot at getting to know him. He was a very strong asset for Kristen, and I would make sure that I let her know it.

Chapter 18

Like Taking Candy From a CFO

As I walked down the hall at United Software, Raj fell in beside me. I'm six feet tall, yet I only came up to his shoulder. I could tell that something was on his mind. "Trouble with your calls?" I asked. "No no, I'm getting better all the time," he answered. "I've got people coming to me for advice now. You really helped me." It sounded like I might have helped myself out of a job. I asked why he looked troubled if he was doing so well. "Well, it's like this . . . ." He started.

Raj relished his status as the premier cold caller in the office. Lately, he'd kicked butt in a couple of informal cold-calling contests. It was all in good fun, but it gave him a reputation in the bullpen that he had never possessed before. If you have ever had the pleasure of working out of a sales bullpen, you know that it is the business equivalent of the high school locker room. It's a little gross, it can be very funny, and it is a lot easier to take if you have a little status in the group. Raj finally had his status, and one of the senior reps had come up with a way to knock him down a little. The senior guy had suckered Raj into accepting a bet that he could get an appointment with the CFO of a particularly desirable potential client. Raj took the bet without realizing that the deck was stacked against him; the senior rep had tried the account and knew that the CFO was impossible to get to. An extremely protective assistant guarded him, and nobody knew of a sales rep from any company that had gotten an appointment with the man himself. When all this came out, the collective assumption was that Raj didn't have a chance and wouldn't even try. Everyone had a laugh, but Raj couldn't sleep at night. It seems that my new friend has a quiet competitive streak.

"Got a dog, Raj?" I asked. He said that he did.

"Don't tell me—It's a bulldog of some sort. Right?" I joked, using my staggering powers of deduction. His dog would have to be tenacious.

"Nope, miniature poodle," he replied humorlessly.

It was time to change the subject. I asked Raj how much he had bet. "One hundred bucks, but it's really not about the money. There *has* to be a way to get this guy to see me."

I thought I had an idea for him. Raj told me he'd take me out for the best dinner in the city if it worked. He would spend more than his hundred, but Raj still thought it would be a good deal.

"You have to position the assistant so that she has no choice but to pass your information to the CFO," I told him. "Then the trick is to get him to pay attention to your message. Fortunately for you, there is a way to do both things at once."

Raj rolled his eyes. "Please, you're killing me. What can I do?"

I told him my plan. I pointed out that even the best trick is still a low-percentage play, and then I gave him the number of my personal chocolatier and told him to have two small chocolate computers molded with the United Software logo rendered in icing on the screen. In the meantime, he should draft a letter to the CFO requesting an appointment.

"Don't be too cute. Be brief and professional. Then put the chocolate computers in a package with the letter and bring it upstairs to Denise Oglethorpe. Tell her I sent you and ask her if, hypothetically, she would pass the chocolate computers through to Kristen if an outside sales person sent them to her. Listen to what she tells you and change the letter if she tells you to. She's a gate keeper just like your prospect's assistant."

Raj thought the idea had a pretty good chance. I asked him to let me know what happened when he spoke with Denise.

"Bart, I don't want you to take offense, but I think she might be a little too classy for you."

I smiled. "That's not a big deal. There are women in the World Wrestling Federation who are a little too classy for me."

"That's my point." He smiled down at me. "They wouldn't date you either."

Chapter 19

Survival of the Most Rejected

I found Manny at his desk working on his forecast. He didn't look as energetic as he usually did. In fact, Manny looked a little older than he did the last time I saw him. I guessed that my feeling about his prospect operating on a different buying schedule than he suspected was correct.

"I feel like a fool, Bart. When I spoke with the VP, he was shocked that I had thought that the buy was now. It turns out the deal is five or six months out. That explains why they weren't projecting any urgency."

I asked him if he had any plans for the account, given what he had learned. He told me that he didn't have anything new to do—he just had a lot more time to do it in.

"I've got to back off the forecast and admit that I was wrong. I'll stay in touch with them until they are ready to get going again in a few months. We'll get the business then," he said dejectedly.

I didn't like what I thought I was hearing. "So you're going to let them go off on their own until they are ready to go into closing mode—and then you'll finish up with the cost justification?"

"Yeah," Manny sighed. "The VP says that they have a lot of internal stuff to go through and that it should take them a few months. I told him that I would keep in touch."

"Manny, is it ok if I give you a few tips?" I asked delicately.

"Sure, you were dead-on last time."

"First, forget about missing the timing issue. It happened, and you'll be careful about it next time. A few people are going to say 'I told you so,' but most of them don't carry quotas and don't know what it's like to go find deals. If you don't go out on a limb and try, you don't get commission checks."

He still looked low. "Well, I'm not going to pick up any commission on this deal anytime soon."

"That's item number two—your attitude. You have a lot of reasons to be low. The company is having management issues, you're having a hard time getting resources, your deal isn't moving as quickly as you would like. There are probably a few more, but it makes me too depressed to think about all of them." That got a small smile and a nod out of him.

"Well, Manny, is somebody going to come in and fix all that?" I was on a roll; all he had time for was a small headshake. "I'm pretty sure that nobody is. In fact, the only way you're going to get out of it is to take responsibility for your own attitude. I've never seen a sales person achieve success at the same time that he's feeling sorry for himself and hinting about quitting. If things are really that bad, you *should* quit. The worst thing you can do is let the job drag you down to the level you're at now. You have a lot of opportunity at United Software and with this account. I think that you would be an idiot to give up on it now."

Manny looked at me as though he was going to give me an argument. I could see him running through what'd I'd said in his head. In the end, he looked down and muttered, "I'm not ready to give up."

"That leads me to item number three. I think you're making a mistake with this prospect." Manny looked up. "If you leave this prospect alone for any period of time, you are going to lose them. The competition is going to find a way in, because the prospect sees you simply as a provider of technology rather than as a business partner. You should use the additional time as an asset and change the nature of your relationship with your prospect."

Manny was intrigued by this idea. He wanted to know how he could change his relationship. I told him that every situation was a little bit different, but that there were certain things he could look at that would be a help to the prospect and improve his standing. Here are some examples of what we talked about.

Bart's Advice on Improving Your Standing with an Account

Call low

The prospect VP is always going to have to rely on experts to advise him. Those experts are often several layers down in the reporting structure. They may even pass their recommendations through intermediaries. Why not use the time you have to find out what their criteria are and make sure you have their endorsement and the endorsements of their managers? If you don't, your competition might. Why risk it?

Call wide

When deals go fast, you worry about the chain of command. When deals slow down, you have the luxury of calling on people who are outside of that chain. By calling on managers and executives that are not part of the initial project, you may find new opportunities to exploit. You may find opposition that you were unaware of that you can neutralize. Best of all, you may find new sources of information and support.

Build your reference sale

It is important to give your prospect the feeling that your solution is technically suited to their business, but that's not enough. You want your prospect to understand that others have used your product and that it worked out well for them. The best way to do this is by reference. Introduce prospects to your existing customers and let them hear first hand how good it is to be your customer. Ask your existing customers to speak specifically about support and quality of service. Competition can always dispute the technical merits of one of your features, but if your prospect is convinced that your company will stand by them when they're having trouble, the competition doesn't stand a chance.

Give them the tough questions

Share information with your prospect. Consider giving them a list of insightful questions that you have been asked by other prospects. Also give them your responses. This is a great way of conveying your thinking about what is right for their account; the questions and answers you provide may wind up being used against your competition.

Prove your interest

Never underestimate the power of showing up. Many people believe that you will disappear after one call. Sales people have this reputation. *You are a sales professional!* Hanging in and developing a relationship over multiple interactions shows that you care and that you are willing to work for the business. You will always need to qualify and spend your time wisely, but realize that one call is usually not enough to impress people.

Use your executives
Don't wait until the deal is closing to introduce your executive to the key players from an account. If you have a quality prospect and some lead-time, have a pre-closing executive meeting. This will establish the beginnings of a relationship that will be invaluable when the deal is ready to close.

Manny hesitated when I mentioned the last point. In his experience, executive calls were disasters that put entire deals at risk. Dave had said the same thing. I told Manny that he was right—but things had changed. Part of changing his attitude would have to be acknowledging that management had changed, too. He would need to be willing to give them another try. The alternative would be to accept defeat. We agreed that he would ask Kristen Archer to join him in a pre-closing call to his prospect. He would write a document summarizing the account and brief her fully on what he wanted from her before the meeting. When Manny left me, he was resolved to change and to create an environment in which he could enjoy his job and be productive. He wasn't nearly as high as he had been when I first met him, but he had a plan of action and a realistic understanding of where he was in his deal. I liked his odds a lot better than I had before. When I got back to my office, I called Denise to arrange for a meeting with Kristen to go over my recommendations. We set the appointment for Friday of that week. Denise told me that Raj had been to see her and that she liked the chocolate computers idea. She thought that she had been of some help in constructing Raj's letter. Our conversation was warm and pleasant. I was delighted with Denise's change in attitude, and took it to be a direct result of my patience and persistence. Of course, it could easily have been the cumulative effects of my charm and good looks as well.

I realize now that I may have made a small tactical error by proposing marriage over the phone at that time. Perhaps Denise enjoys a more traditional and personal approach and would have preferred an email or instant message. In any event, I took some encouragement from the fact that calling me a "colossal jerk" is not quite the same as saying no.

Chapter 20

Zombie Sales Wisdom

My talk with Manny left me thinking about how people deal with competition. Most people hate it, but true sales professionals have a more nuanced view. They realize that competition broadens markets for growth companies. Imagine that Manny's company has invented a new category of computer, one that you wear as a hat. Manny's company is small, but it owns one hundred percent of the market! Great, huh? Not so much. Because the market is tiny!

One day Manny wakes up to read that Giganto-Mega Computer has announced the Chapeau 1000C cranial computer. Everybody starts talking about hat computing. All of the sudden, Manny's company sees a huge drop in market share; they are at fifty percent of the market and falling. Luckily, the market has quadrupled in size overnight. That means that Manny sees his sales volume double! All because his dreaded competition educated the market for him. His company grows like crazy. Sometimes it is hard to hate the competition.

Today, Manny looks at competition as something dreadful. He may be right in that he could lose his deal and that would be bad. He needs to do all the things I told him about to prepare for the competition, but he needs to change his attitude as well. Prospects can smell fear like a stinky cologne.

How to Benefit from Competition

Understand it

Your competition has a message and a point of view about their products, customers, and the market. If you understand it, you can help your prospect understand how your offering is different and better. You will also be able to identify what part of your prospect's thinking, if any, originates from the competition, and react to it. This will improve your communication with your prospect.

Get an edge

You don't want to lose. Consider what your competition is doing and use it as motivation to get off your butt and do something great for your customer. If you don't, the competition will.

Agree

There are probably a lot of points that you agree with your competitors about. Don't be afraid to acknowledge them. Honestly agreeing with your competition will improve your standing with the prospect by proving your honesty and maturity. Disagreeing with everything they say appears petty and self-interested.

Meet the competition

What have you got to lose? What could you learn? Maybe things aren't so great for them. Studies that I made up have found that they will ask you if there are openings at your company an astounding 25.3% of the time!

Eat their brains

Everyone knows that killing your competition and eating their brains is an effective way of making their talents and knowledge your own. But this method introduces culinary challenges and, in some states, legal restrictions. Please consult with local authorities before using this approach.

I was pretty sure that Manny's attitude would evolve. He was a smart, hardworking guy, and he didn't seem to be unusually fearful. Manny was becoming a sales professional. Sometimes Business Detectives just worry too much.

Chapter 21

The Best Place I've Been Thrown Out Of

I had two days before my meeting with Kristen. That was enough time to prepare for the presentation properly. I had to convince her that I understood and had correctly diagnosed the problems at United Software. Kristen knew that she had problems—my challenge would be to explain how those problems were related, and how the most important ones all came back to one central issue. Once I accomplished that, I would have to convince Kristen that I had a system that would address the problem. She needed to believe in the solution strongly enough to commit to following the program herself and to coax, cajole, or compel the rest of her team to do the same. It wasn't going to be easy, so I prepared the best way I knew how: I had beers with John.

I described my approach to John over the course of the evening. John played Kristen Archer, which gave new meaning to the phrase "against nature." Fortunately, I'm a professional and was able to stay focused on the task at hand. My case was compelling. My presentation captured the essence of what I wanted to convey, and balanced upon the razor edge between high drama and down-to-earth practicality. John was moved, and declared that Kristen would have no choice but to see the brilliance of the assessment and follow every one of my recommendations to the letter. He even mused that there should be a monument to me and my faithful sidekick erected in the lobby of the building. John's humility was inspiring. At that point Sarah came out of the kitchen and announced that we were drunk and disturbing the other customers. "I'm calling you both cabs and tossing your sodden carcasses out of here," she declared for the entire bar to hear.

Several patrons muttered approval or raised their glasses in salute. None of the wretches came to our aid.

"Aw, now honey, Bart and I are going to help you clean up the kitchen," John cooed.

"You two would be even less help than usual. You'd probably end up drowning in the sink." And with that, she hustled us out the door. I barely had time to salute the moose with my fedora on the way out. We were moving fast, but I think he may have replied that time.

I went to work on my presentation in earnest the next day and stayed at it until the evening before my meeting. For some reason, I'd lost the brilliant phrasing and laser-sharp rejoinders that had come so easily the night before at the bar with John—and I'd gained a headache. On the other hand, I found myself lacking any interest in going out for a beer break. I was able to concentrate on preparing for the meeting.

Chapter 22

Everyone Loves Them But the Alpaca

Friday dawned with the promise of greatness in the city that seldom buys. I rolled out of bed in plenty of time to see it. After two hundred pushups and an ice-cold shower complete with loofah, I dressed for the day. I selected a gray pinstripe suit with very lightly padded shoulders and a white shirt with tab collar. My tie picked up the pinstripe, but my shoes were the real showstoppers.

I pulled out my Anselmo Carbonara loafers. They were constructed by hand from the nether regions of alpacas that were only allowed to sleep on air mattresses and were raised exclusively on radicchio and cabernet. These shoes were made with soles so thin that you could read the society column through them. I did not. I only wore them for big appointments, as they required a level of maintenance usually reserved for British motor vehicles.

I slammed down a couple of lattes on my way to United Software. When I arrived, I discovered that Fridays were casual days. I looked like an idiot. Denise wore a button-down shirt and a blue blazer, managing to make it look like the latest design from Milan. Given my regrettable marriage proposal of a few days earlier, I decided to keep my opinion to myself until after the meeting.

A few minutes before the meeting, Denise settled me into Kristen's office. Glancing around the place, you wouldn't know that she was under any pressure at all. Other than a few things she was probably working on that morning littering her desk, the place was perfect. I suspected that Kristen's office wouldn't show the strain even if the company collapsed. That could be because of Kristen or because Denise would not allow it.

Probably both.

Kristen was right on time, as always. We chatted for a few minutes. Her daughter Erin played soccer, and her team was playing for the championship that weekend. We both thought that the tiny orange fish eggs were the best part of going for sushi. The small talk was brief, because we both wanted to get down to business.

The meeting went on for hours. Kristen wasn't taking anything I said for granted, and she wasn't trying to sharp-shoot me either. She realized that her business future — and her company's — depended on what she ultimately decided to do, so she drilled into the problem. I started by laying out the problem areas that I found and assessing each one.

Chapter 23

The Simple Truth

I began with the basics. United Software had forgotten the fundamental rule of feature, function, and benefit. Kristen balked at this one right away. She pointed out that every relevant piece of collateral carefully described the product's features and tied them to how a client could use them and what benefits they would derive. I told her that she was right, but the problem wasn't with the literature—it was with the people. More specifically, it was with how the company was training the people. I identified several cases in which sales people were listing benefits without first establishing feature and function. This meant that potential prospects were likely to get frustrated and stop working with the sales people before any real sales relationship could be established. We talked at length about Raj's difficulties and what I had done to get him back on track.

"It's just basic sales management," I explained. "When you get yourself a decent VP of sales, he or she will pick up on it right away. It shows up in the rate of addition to your pipeline and the hit rate against the leads that marketing is passing to sales."

"Should we be hiring different sales people?" she wondered.

"Not because of this." I told her. "While the effect of this problem can be serious, the cause and the fixes are really pretty simple. Get a sharp sales management team, emphasize good basic sales skills in training, and reinforce those skills once people are in the field. I'd start with new employee training and move out from there."

"We could start to do that right away."

"Yes, and you should. When I had inquiry calls made to your sales offices, the responses we got were pretty bad. It's not just Raj or his office. I think that improving your sales people's ability to respond appropriately to inquiries will show up in pipeline growth within a couple of months."

Kristen thought some more. "How did this happen, and why didn't we catch it before? "I told her it was a lot like her daughter's soccer team. It wouldn't matter if the kids had the fanciest moves in the world if they forgot how to pass and shoot. The problem is that even good players forget to execute the basics all the time. It's up to the coaches to teach and practice the fundamental skills necessary to win. At United

Software, the people who were supposed to be coaching had missed a basic problem. Now they were gone, and Kristen would have to fill their role personally or get someone else to do it.

Chapter 24

The Truth is Rarely Simple

Kristen asked what I thought of the lead-generation program that marketing had going. Even though she left her role as VP of marketing behind, I knew that this point was a little sensitive. She did not want to believe that her efforts in marketing had been in vain. Luckily, they hadn't.

"Every sales person that I met complained about the quality of the leads they received," I told Kristen. Her mouth set into a hard line. Before she could respond, I went on. "That was my first hint that there was a bigger problem. Even if the leads truly were terrible, there should have been a little bit of a variety in people's opinion about them. But everyone was in agreement. I knew they were dead wrong."

Kristen didn't really look angry now—just confused. "Wouldn't that just tell you that the leads were terrible?"

"No, it told me that someone had worked to unify the opinion."

"What?" She looked incredulous.

"The opinion was universal. Somebody wanted to make sure that the marketing leads were viewed negatively. My guess is that it was the previous VP of sales, and he did it for political reasons. You were pretty clear that he wanted the top job and was determined to get it."

"Yes, he wanted it. This is surprising." Her eyes seemed to get darker. I wondered how she did that.

"He was probably concerned about you looking too good, so he started talking about how your department was ineffective. I suspect he lobbied the outgoing president, hoping that he would have influence with the board."

"And when the president just walked out, it backfired and the board chose me."

I smiled. "I'm sure there were a lot of good solid reasons for choosing you, but this may explain some of the politics."

It was her turn to smile. "Bart, if this project were for me personally you would have just earned your exorbitant fee, but I can't believe that politics is the only thing going on with the leads."

"It's not—and my fees are very reasonable. Remember that we made test calls to the sales offices. Those are essentially leads that came around marketing to sales. I told you that the pitches were weak and we spoke about what to do about it, but there was a larger problem."

"I know it's your job to find the problems, but if we don't take a break soon I'm going to hit you with a chair." Thankfully, she laughed as she said this. "Go on."

"The problem was that we didn't get a lot callbacks. We made 25 calls, yet only 17 were returned."

"Ouch."

"Yeah, it seems that the sales people don't have a very clear understanding of territories. I think that it's basically an administrative issue. You should be able to get control of it by working with the district managers to make sure there are controls in place and that leads don't fall through the cracks."

"OK, that sounds reasonable. But what do you recommend I do about the negative view of the leads?"

"Well, that's a little trickier. You're dealing with perception, emotion, and a little bit of inertia—because someone was pushing people in the other direction. I'd look at a few things."

Bart's Advice on Changing Attitudes

Make it clear to the managers that there is a problem and that fixing it is the only acceptable solution. The managers need to understand that playing politics with any other department is not a winning strategy. Straight talk is your best weapon here. Don't be surprised if the worst offenders are the first to turn around. Their offenses might have been in response to what they saw as the political reality of the past. Explaining the new reality might make them very happy.

Reward the people who change. Find a way to identify the people who are getting the most out of the leads that they're already getting—and reward them with more leads. New hires are a great place to look, because they need the leads to get started and they aren't influenced by the old culture yet.

Emphasize capitalism! Recognize the people who make progress. Their compensation plans will take care of them financially, but don't hesitate to use public praise to reinforce your message.

Watch out for a backlash. Marketing folks might decide that they have won, and they might cop an attitude. Keep an eye out. This isn't about groups winning or losing; it's about getting deals. Maybe you can find a way to reward them for generating leads that come through. The reward does not have to be financial.

Kristen thought that my suggested steps were reasonable. She was ready to go a little further with incentives than I would have recommended, but that was a small difference. I always argue for letting the main compensation plan be the driver for sales behavior and using very small adjustments. In my experience, CEOs prefer bolder action. I can't really criticize that approach too severely; it's usually their job that is on the line.

We took a break, and Kristen asked Denise to order lunch. I thought about trying to impress Denise with my exemplary dietary habits, but decided that I wasn't doing very well in trying to impress her. I asked for a recently dead mammal encased in pieces of a baked, wheat-based starch formulation. With mayonnaise.

Chapter 25

Simple Does Not Mean Easy

After the break, we got ready for the big stuff. I told Kristen that there were a lot of individual symptoms at United Software, and she could try and address each one separately. But she would go crazy trying to track all the problems, and she was very likely to undo the fix for one problem with the fix for the next. What we were looking for was one core flaw that tied a bunch of issues together. If we could identify that, we would make progress.

"I suspect you have that answer," she said archly.

I think that I do, but your opinion is the one that matters. Let's talk about some individual issues first, and then I'll try to tie them all together. After that, we can discuss a solution."

"Go ahead."

"First, let's go back and look at Raj's problems again." I explained that Raj had bigger problems than just failing to establish feature, function, and benefit with his prospects. He had almost nothing showing up on any forecasts, even though he worked like a dog. As a result, a promising young guy and his prospect were getting almost no management attention, and the company was at risk of losing both the employee and the deals.

"It's not just one guy?" Kristen asked.

"No, it's not. As an example, Manny Rodriguez has a similar problem with different symptoms. He has trouble getting resources for his deals, so he winds up forecasting them higher than they should be. Dave Pelton, on the other hand, thinks his deals have gotten too much management attention, so he under-forecasts like crazy."

"Why don't I just come down on these guys like a ton of bricks?"

"Well, you might need to at some point, but let's look at some of the other issues that might tie in." I am a gifted diplomat.

She shook her head. "I should have guessed that there was more."

I told her more about the test calls that John had made. I explained how some of the calls didn't get returned, but the ones that did wound up in the forecast. Some were at an appropriately low level; after all, the calls were just polite inquiries, and we did our best to disqualify ourselves as prospects as soon as we spoke with a sales person. But other calls wound up being forecasted very high. I explained that the calls probably should not have even appeared on the forecast, but that there was no way they should appear with a high probability of close. Then I told her the worst of it: when we compared the field version of the forecast to the executive version, some of John's calls had been moved up in probability. Since we had originated the inquiries, we knew that it was completely wrong to move them up.

"Do you mean that I have people purposely lying to me?" She looked like she was thinking about hitting me with a chair again.

"I can certainly understand your coming to that conclusion, but I think that you should look at the whole picture. Remember how the sales people are inconsistent with their forecasts, and how some tend to inflate and some tend to deflate?"

Kristen was quick. "So sales administration and the managers are trying to adjust for their sales people, and blowing it?"

"That's my theory." I told her.

"What a mess! What else do I need to know?"

"You pretty well have it. Your forecasts are approaching useless. That's bad enough for predicting revenue, but its worse in terms of applying management and technical resource. The problem goes all the way down to your first-level managers. They are pretty much flying blind."

"Do you have a prognosis?"

"Your performance will continue to be unpredictable with a declining trend. At some point, the frustration that people are feeling will boil over, and you'll start to have serious employee turnover problems. I've gotten a few hints that people are unhappy already, so I'm guessing that you'll start to see people quitting within a couple of months."

She was shocked. She knew that United Software had problems, but I don't think that she anticipated the depth of the issues. We broke for lunch, and when I returned from a particularly long restroom visit she explained that she would have hunted me down and dragged me back to her office had I attempted to leave before we worked through the solution part of the problems.

I had more or less given up on Denise. On my way back into Kristen's office, I thanked her for the mammal sandwich. She must have sensed that I had stopped pursuing her, because she was much easier to talk to. I don't think she insulted me once. Kristen, however, was all pumped up. We got right back to it.

"All right, Bart. You spent the morning pushing my head under water. How about throwing me a life preserver?"

"I think my solution is more like the two of us building a boat. We have to work fast before everybody drowns. The first thing for us to do is agree on what the common thread is."

"That's easy," she said. "A total lack of discipline."

"Good point. I'll bet your kids never miss curfew," I answered.

She grinned at that. "Erin did . . . once."

"Well, I'd guess you're a pretty good parent, and that you don't govern on punishment alone. What else goes into discipline?"

She puzzled for a minute. "My kids know the rules, they know what is expected of them, because my expectations are consistent."

Bingo. "I think that's what's missing at United Software. The rules of forecasting are weak and inconsistent and, if you look at it over time, they have changed from one management regime to another. I'd suggest that you need to lay out workable rules before you try to enforce them."

Kristen objected. "These are adults! Why can't they understand that they need to forecast accurately?

Every company in the world does forecasts. Why should this one be any different?"

"But you *are* getting a forecast and, from what I can see, you get it on time."

"But it's total crap!" She was having a hard time getting my point.

"Yeah, it is. But that's because you don't have a universally acknowledged way to measure deals. Your people evaluate accounts, but management can't tell what they mean. Each part of management "adds value" by trying to interpret the input, and by the time it gets to you, it is worse than useless — it's misleading. All of your automated sales systems just help to churn out meaningless information faster."

Kristen was still fighting, but I could see she was starting to catch on. "Are you trying to say that the millions we spent on automation have to be scrapped?"

"No, of course not. You have a great automated system, and if you fix this problem it can help you recover very quickly. What you can't do is rely on the technology alone. There needs to be a solid management system and a method for evaluating prospects that goes with it."

Kristen went silent. I placed a bet with myself that she would acknowledge the problem and take one more run at me before we could get to work on the solution. I won. I owed myself a beer.

"I guess I can see what you're saying, but I'm not going to spend hundreds of thousands of dollars buying the 'lethargic selling' program or the one where the guy explains how corporate sales is exactly like landing a jet on an aircraft carrier," she said.

"I always liked 'Sales Secrets of the CIA' myself. But no, I'm not advocating buying into some expensive program. I just want you to move from *subjective* prospect evaluation to *objective* prospect evaluation."

Kristen asked me to expand on this. I explained that the way it worked now, all the sales people evaluated prospects on their percentage chance of closing in the current quarter. This was a subjective measure, and there were some serious problems with it. First, it was often a better reflection of the sales person's mood than anything else. Some people forecast too high, some too low. There was no reference point to reality in the system. Second, some managers tried to apply qualifying criteria to match the percentages. But hybrid systems like that break because management is mixing two ways of evaluating together and asking the sales person to take responsibility for making the correct judgment. For example, a deal might be in the contracts phase, but doesn't necessarily mean that it has an eighty percent chance of closing in a month. The sales person can't be forced to resolve the conflict, because it results in the unreliability that was making management so difficult and the sales people so unhappy.

What I wanted United Software to do was to abandon the subjective, percentage-chance-of-close method that they were used to and switch to an objective measurement. I recommended establishing a ranking system of ten sales stages based purely on pre-established criteria. For example, a prospect could not be ranked at a nine unless there was a purchase order authorized and in process. To give a deal this rating, the sales person should be able to explain exactly where that PO was, when it was due to the company, and how she knows that. Each stage would have a similar set of clear, concise criteria.

"Isn't a forecast supposed to tell you when the deals will close?"

"Remember that you really don't want your sales reps doing a forecast. You have everything that anybody in the company needs sitting right in your automated system. In fact, I would argue that you could do away with forecasts all together. Sales administration can do a run against the system periodically and then the appropriate management can review the results. The results will display the sales stage as well as the expected close date. What will be missing is the percentage."

"Doesn't that defeat the purpose?"

"Not at all. You will quickly build a history that says how many deals you need at a particular ranking at a given time in your quarter or year to deliver a certain dollar volume," I told her. "You can use the expected close date and other information as a cross check."

"So what is the advantage?"

I smiled. "There are bunches. Because your sales people are using objective criteria, they are less likely to inflate or deflate. Managers can ask meaningful questions about prospects to help accurately assess them. They can help sales teams evaluate how to move prospects from a '1' to a '2' or from a '7' to an '8.' Everyone will know what they mean. Sales administration can generate analyses about when it is time to progress and to close. You will be able to look into sales' operations and spot best practices and dangerous problems. Even better, managers will begin to see where to apply resources.

"It fixes everything?"

"No. This isn't a panacea. What this will do is give you a common language for talking about sales across your company. When somebody describes a prospect, there will be a defined meaning to the description. That can be the foundation for good management to fix problems and improve efficiency."

"What would the company have to do to make a change like this?" she wondered.

"There would be very little in hard costs. Perhaps some small changes to your sales force automation system. You might also have some training and meeting costs. The biggest cost would be intangible. There is no way to do this in phases or as an experiment, and it is a big cultural change. You would have to get behind the project and get all of the key managers behind it, too."

"Then you expect it to be difficult?" she asked.

"Yes, at first. Some of the problem is just resistance. More of the problem is learning. Everyone has to learn the new system and get used to working that way. The worst of it will be over in a couple of weeks, but you have to stay on top of it for a couple of months until it gets to be habit for everybody."

"Well, Bart, I'm interested. But I'm still a little skeptical. I want to understand the sales stages and I want to get opinions from some other people within the company." We agreed that we would resume the next day, and that she would have four additional people with her. I would catch them up on the discussion and then run through my proposed sales stages and the requirements for each one. Kristen would fill them in a little beforehand when she called them to ruin their Saturday plans. Since it would be Saturday, we would start at eight thirty and wrap it up by eleven. I got her to agree to have everyone meet at the Elegant Moose Pub. We would have the place to ourselves, and the team members could get a good breakfast and a change of scenery.

When I left, Denise was away from her desk. I had stopped caring.

Chapter 26

Paying a Debt

I walked into the Moose at about three o'clock. Sarah had gone to the bank and would be back in about fifteen minutes. I had called John to let him know I was on my way, but he was busy. Lewis was Sarah's bartender and sometime piano player. He poured me a lager in a frosted mug. I'd won it from myself back in Kristen's office, and I always pay my debts.

It was fourteen minutes later and my eyes were closed when I smelled something sweet and felt soft hands rubbing my shoulders.

"If this is what I get for just having a beer in your place, what's the going rate for setting you up with a business breakfast?"

"How about I just buy you another beer? My boyfriend is an insanely jealous haberdasher. He might dress you badly," Sarah purred.

"And charge me too much for it. I'll take the beer, no offense."

"You, Mr. Steele, are easily intimidated. What's the deal?" I explained that I'd be bringing five people in the next day for an early breakfast. Sarah started worrying about what to serve—she didn't normally do breakfast—but she had wanted to get some corporate business for a while and this would be a good start. She left for the kitchen. I looked around the place and wondered if I had done the right thing. It was a nice bar, in that sawdust-on-the-floor kind of way, but it wasn't the Ritz. I said goodbye to the moose and left. No reply. Some ungulates have no manners.

Chapter 27

A Moose in the Morning

I have been accused of paying too much attention to my appearance. I realize that this is ridiculous, but I now decline to dress for business on Saturdays in order to avoid this kind of small-minded accusation. I ran an easy six miles and through the drive-thru espresso shop on the way home. An hour later I arrived at the Elegant Moose Pub in my Reeboks, torn up Levi's, and my favorite long-sleeved Bare Naked Ladies concert t-shirt. Nothing on my body had ever crossed an ocean.

The pub was transformed. What was merely comfortable by night was charming in the morning. Sarah had hit the farmers market, and the place bloomed with flowers and greens. The shades were up and the sunshine revealed a large table with a checked tablecloth and heavy ceramic pitchers full of hand-squeezed juice. This combined with the sawdust on the floor gave the place a country feel. It smelled of fresh-baked bread and coffee. If they serve breakfast in heaven, Sarah will run it one day.

Kristen arrived first and went wild over the place. Sarah hustled her off for a tour of the kitchen. It looked to me that Sarah would be entertaining corporate guests more often. The others arrived shortly. Kristen had selected the head of sales administration; her replacement in marketing; Rob Lazlo, the district manager; and Dave Pelton, United Software's top sales person.

Breakfast was terrific. I used the time to repeat what I had explained to Kristen the day before. Everyone took it pretty well. It was clear that Kristen had spent some time with each person. The sales administration guy acted a little bit sheepish. I suspected that Kristen had mentioned her views on the quality of the forecast and the possibility that his department had been raising the probability on deals. Dave was OK. I was a little worried that he would resent getting exposed for keeping his forecast low, but he seemed content. When I wrapped up, I asked if there were any questions or comments.

Rob Lazlo piped up first. "It sounds great, but I'm worried that deals will drag on forever because the sales people won't feel accountable anymore."

"If you do this correctly, you'll have *more* accountability from the sales professionals," I told him. "With the objective sales stage system in place, you will be able to specifically question whether or not a prospect is ranked correctly. You can drill into the account in a way that you never could with an estimate of the percentage of close."

"I'll bet the sales folks will love that," said the marketing VP.

I turned to Dave. "What about it?"

Dave didn't hesitate. "If the sales person is any good they'll love it. We had to play politics with the forecast for a long time. That doesn't help get deals closed. It just takes away from selling time."

The guy from sales administration didn't seem convinced. "I'm worried that we won't have anybody on the hook for the forecast any more."

"I don't think that the responsibility really shifts very much. Sales people must accurately rank their prospects, and managers should be pulling reports and going over them with the sales people to make sure they are accurate. In reviews, executives should be drilling into the more highly ranked deals to make sure they hold up. The responsibility is still there, but the process is more objective and there is a common set of terms and expectations for everyone to work from."

I can't say that I saw acceptance at that point, but the resistance was low. I could see that everyone in the group needed to get an idea of what the objective ranking criteria would be. I spent the next hour and a half working my way through my ideas. I started by explaining that I was going to present a ranking system that other companies I worked with had used with success. Each company wound up changing and adjusting the rankings somewhat, and that was fine. Some added an eleventh stage to show that the deal was done and off the forecast. It didn't matter what the stages were, as long as they accurately represented United Software's sale cycle and the company adopted the practice and discipline of using them. Everyone said that they understood.

Chapter 28

Ten Stages

No one fell asleep. I took the group through each of the ten sales ranking stages, discussing what each one meant in the context of the sales process. Here are the notes that I passed out for them to work from.

Assessing Prospects

Sales Stage Guidelines

The following notes are intended to help you rank prospects and be prepared for management questions at each stage. Each prospect is unique, and your prospect situation may deviate from the stage ranking. If you choose to rank a prospect ahead of the criteria for the appropriate stage, please notify sales management so that we can understand why and preserve the integrity of the pipeline.

The criteria in the sales stage rankings apply to prospects that you are working with directly or in conjunction with a partner company. Partner prospects may tend to enter the pipeline at a higher stage due to the work that the partner company has done before we were alerted to the prospect. If you are working with a partner, ensure that the answers that you get to your qualifying questions are based on direct information that the partner has received from the prospect—not suppositions or assumptions. By doing this, you will obtain useful information and assist your partner in closing the prospect as quickly as possible.

1. Potential sales opportunity

To achieve this ranking and enter the pipeline, the prospect must have given us some positive indication of their interest. They may have called or emailed us or returned a response card by mail. They might have indicated their interest to a partner. The target is merely a suspect until they reach this qualification. You might want to track a suspect in the sales automation system, but a suspect should not be given this rating until they have given you some positive feedback.

2. Application area identified

The prospect reached the first stage by giving you positive feedback. In this second stage, you know how the prospect might use United Software's product. You should have an idea as to *why* they gave you positive feedback. Expect management to ask you questions like: What is the prospect's business need? Where are your contacts in the organization? How big is the organization? If possible, you should look at their web site or another resource to begin to understand their business.

3. One of several contenders

You have met the criteria in stage three, and the prospect has begun to understand the benefits of your product. The other contenders for their business may be direct competition, or they may be alternative ways of doing business such as hiring temporary staff. The important point, and what moves them into this stage, is that the prospect is actively evaluating alternatives.

4. Active in known buying process

The key decision maker has been identified. This could be one person or more than one. If it is more than one, it is important to know who each person is and what his or her role will be. You should be able to answer questions like: Is the prospect aware of approximate system pricing? Is a cost justification necessary? Do they have a defined level of justification that we will need to achieve? Are there established evaluation criteria? What is the timeline for purchase?

5. Finalist in competitive sale

This stage is characterized by 2nd and 3rd demonstrations as well as detailed functionality and usage questions. If the deal warrants an on-site demonstration, it is likely to occur at this stage. This is also a great stage at which to use expert resources that may be available to you. Again, the competition may be other product vendors or alternative ways of doing business.

6. Favored vendor

At this stage, your prospect contacts are telling you that they want your solution over the alternatives. You may be helping them work on a justification package or a presentation to senior management. The key question is: Who has told you that you are favored?

7. Funds allocated, timeline confirmed
At this stage, the prospect has told you that the funds have been allocated for spending with your company. They have also confirmed their purchase timing.

8. Negotiating contract
The prospect should have the purchase or lease agreement at any earlier stage. In this stage, the customer has expressed any objections and you are working with the prospect and management to resolve them. Management will ask you if you know who at the prospect's operation has final approval of terms, and you should know the answer to this question.

9. PO in process
Negotiations of terms have reached a conclusion, and the prospect is engaged in the process of issuing a PO and/or signing the contract. You are expected to be able to describe this process in painstaking detail— over and over again.

10. PO issued
The purchase order is in your possession. This may be a customer PO or the resultant partner PO. Regardless, you have it clutched in your sweaty little hand.

When I'd finished laying out the process, Kristen looked confused. "After all the talk, I was expecting something more dramatic. I think that we are pretty much doing this already."

Again, I turned to Dave. He didn't let me down. "No, Kristen, we're not. Our current process asks me when a prospect is going to close and how confident I am about it. This process asks me specific details about what is going on in my account."

"Aren't these rankings so easy that they're trivial? Don't you do them every day without thinking about it?" she pressed.

Before Dave could answer, Rob Lazlo jumped in. "I don't think that it is trivial. I think that it's basic. We should be doing it every day. What this process does is help us to see our prospects clearly. You are probably right that we should be doing it without thinking about it, but many people are not, and nobody is giving the information to the company."

"Rob's right. It's all about executing the basics well. It is simple, but it isn't necessarily easy. The whole company will need to change to make this happen," I put in.

The conversation went on like this for a while. Kristen polled her people, and they all agreed that she should follow my recommendations. Dave and Rob were a little bit enthusiastic; the others said that it was the best option in a bad situation. Kristen stayed behind for a few minutes after her people had left.

"Bart, I'm going to do what you suggest, but I have to tell you that it is kind of a desperation move. I don't have a lot of other choices."

"Even so, you're going to need to throw everything you've got at it."

"I will, and the company will. I assume that you will help us get rolling?"

"Of course."

"Then let's start Monday. We don't have any time to waste."

With that, Kristen left. I said goodbye to Sarah, and headed out to think about how we should get started on Monday. I waved to the moose on the way out. I think he smiled.

Chapter 29

Insight Leads to Hard Work — And Progress

The next couple of weeks were a blur. Kristen was as good as her word. She threw everything she had at making the change. When a few sales people were difficult, she pulled them aside and got them back on track. She insisted on using the rankings in every sales discussion she had. That forced the managers to use the new method, and they made sure that the sales people were following it too. Unfortunately, the fresh look that they got at the sales pipeline wasn't very pretty. Even so, for the first time in a long time, it was accurate.

At first, United Software had to use my guesses at how long it would take to move a deal from each stage to the next and at how many deals could be expected to drop out. Later, the sales administration team started to adjust my times to reflect what they were beginning to see in their operation. The process was taking hold.

Raj caught me in the hall one day and started pumping my hand and thanking me. I had to slow him down so that I could understand what he was talking about.

"Mr. Steele — Bart, it worked! I got in to see the CFO at the company I'd placed the bet about. I used the chocolate computers like you told me to, and he said that I had to be smart and that I earned the appointment. I see him next week!"

"That's great. You must feel pretty good. What is it ranked?"

"It's just a "1" until I talk to him, but I have high hopes. This new system is terrific! I've got one deal all the way up to a '7 — Funds allocated, timeline confirmed' and a couple more are coming up quick. You watch, I'll be Rookie of the Year this year. Oh! I owe you dinner. I'll get you a certificate or something."

"I'm glad you're doing so well. I'll trade the dinner for lunch with you in a few weeks. I want to hear about all your deals."

I got away quickly before Raj broke into song.

Chapter 30

Contentment is Often Upside Down

I sat at my desk with my feet up on the windowsill. Things had settled down at United Software, and I was starting to think about my next job when Kristen called. The sun was just dropping behind the warehouse across the street as I stared out the window. "We picked up orders from Dave and Manny today, so I thought I'd call you and let you know. I don't think we would have gotten Manny's deal without your system. For the first time, our sales don't seem like the mystery they used to."

"Congratulations. How's the company doing?"

"Not great, but I'm convinced the worst is over. We're able to do things to try to improve the situation now that we understand it a little better. Rob Lazlo resigned. He said he believed in what we were doing, but he felt too worn out by the previous problems to keep up the fight. I'm disappointed. We could use his experience."

"Too bad. But I always appreciate someone who knows himself well enough to understand when he needs to walk away," I suggested.

"I suppose you're right. I know I have trouble seeing anyone give up."

"Have you convinced Dave to take a manager's job yet?" I asked her, and as I did, I smelled something wonderful and felt soft hands slide over my shoulders and around my neck from behind.

"Not yet, but I will. How am I doing at convincing you to be our VP of sales?" she asked.

I told her that the job wasn't for me. We promised to talk again soon. The sun had disappeared entirely now, and my office was getting dark. As I hung up the phone, I leaned straight back in my chair and was given an interesting upside-down kiss. "It's dark. I have no idea who you are." I said.

The lights came on and revealed Denise Oglethorpe. She had come straight from the office, and was wearing a pinstripe business suit with a silk blouse. Every time I saw her, my chest hurt.

"Your sense of humor never fails to make me hungry. Let's go eat." So we did. That's the story of United Software. Good people were learning to succeed professionally. Some of them were hanging out at the Moose and becoming my friends. The whole story is true—except for when I said that I gave up on Denise. Business Detectives never give up.

About the Author

Brian Schlosser is only 73% as grouchy as his picture. He is a software executive. From time to time he consults with companies facing various turn-around and growth issues.

Brian's interest in company growth developed during his time as CEO of Attenex Corporation and CEO and founder of InterImage Inc. Brian also served in leadership roles at

ImageTag, Motiva, FileNET, DatStat and Imagechoice. Unsurprisingly, the topic of growth came up at these companies too.

Brian lives in Sammamish, Washington with his wife Denise and daughters Kristen and Erin. He cooks, wood carves, and follows his family around when they let him.

Brian spends his free time sleeping or staring blankly into space.